SECRET
KANSAS CITY

A Guide to the Weird, Wonderful, and Obscure

Anne Kniggendorf

Library of Congress Control Number: 2020937362

ISBN: 9781681062839

Front cover: All photos courtesy of the author.
Back cover: Cow—courtesy of Henry Kniggendorf; Tree—courtesy of Dylan Mortimer, author headshot—Brandon Parigo.

Design by Jill Halpin

All photos courtesy of the author unless otherwise noted.

Printed in the United States of America
20 21 22 23 24 5 4 3 2

For my mother and lifelong adventure partner,
Rosemary Kniggendorf

With special thanks to Henry Kniggendorf for
your company on many long drives

And further special thanks to Stephen, Ellis, and Fred Kniggendorf,
for your love, ride-alongs, and edits. Thanks as well to Leslie,
Duane, Arlo, and Juniper Cunningham for jumping in wherever
you could help.

CONTENTS

ACKNOWLEDGMENTS

Writing this book would have been much more difficult without suggestions and research help. Many friends, family members, acquaintances, organizations, and complete strangers contributed wonderful insights and tips for this project. I tried to keep a list, and I'm very sorry if I have missed anyone. They were, in no particular order:

The Cass County Public Library, Terra Hulett, Pat Gray, the Wyandotte County Museum, Janet E. Cunningham, Jason Roe, John Byrd, Mark Reynolds, Linda Coffey, Angelique Dilmore, Todd Anthony Engle, Sherry Wyatt Shinkle, Barbara Pendleton, Phil Weeter, Bill Worley, Chris Wolff, the Jackson County Historical Society, Amy Ayars, Sarah Bader-King, Kathy Reno, Nancy Mays, the Kansas City (Kansas) Public Library, Jaime Picken, Stacy Lawson, the Johnson County Public Library, Julie Denesha, LaDene Morton, Dani Wellemeyer at the UMKC Library, Ann McFerrin, Molly Hutson, Gerald Hay, Robert Swisher, Jeffrey Jennings, Stacy Davidson, Sarah Bader-King, KCUR's Central Standard team, Christian Mancinelli, Debbie Robinson, Cole Klawuhn, Jerry VanAlst, Bryan Stalder, the Local Kansas City History Buffs Facebook page, Karla Deel, Amber Arnett-Bequeaith, Trevor Hoag, Denice Ferguson, Gary Keshner, Anne Deuschle, WenDee Rowe, and Erin Dodson, and all those whose names are included in the stories. Thank you!

INTRODUCTION

Kansas City is a pretty open and welcoming place. Neither locals nor visitors seem to think of the town as cagey, shadowy, dark, or secretive. But not even Kansas City's biggest fan can know everything about this metropolis of 500,000—2.34 million counting the surrounding suburbs, and we do. Think of the city like, I don't know, the Hereford bull way up on his pylon next to I-35: most likely you've seen him, but what do you really know about him? Do you know that his sculptor made him anatomically correct? Probably not, because he spends all his time up in the sky. Or maybe you want to think of the city like Kansas's only Kentucky Derby winner: he's sleek and fast, but at the end of his life, he wound up in a cul-de-sac—that'll make more sense to you later.

But, listen, your fair city is full of many unexpected and hidden jewels, and this volume is just one native daughter's curated collection of them. Is it all-inclusive? Not possible. Would you have included the largest snake in the world, a pink tree, or so many references to books? Perhaps not. But, I'll tell you right now that you'd definitely jump at the chance to tell others about the ghosts you've met, the various experimental societies you've run across, and, best of all, the very plain fact that according to three different groups, Kansas City is endorsed by a higher power as the absolute best place in the country to ride out nearly any type of apocalyptic scenario.

Let me be the first to welcome you to Secret Kansas City. Whether you're just passing through or playing tourist in your own backyard, make a scavenger hunt of finding each and every location. It may take years, but that's okay! When you visit a spot, take a picture and #SecretKansasCity to @AnneKniggendorf on your favorite social media platform.

IMAGINE A WORLD WITHOUT SQUIRRELS

You say you had to purchase them?

A 1915 biography of William Rockhill Nelson mentions, without explanation, that the *Kansas City Star*'s original owner "imported squirrels from adjoining states and turned them loose in the parks to add to their attractiveness and to ruralize them." Wait, was that really necessary?

Whether you live in Midtown, near Westport, or out in the suburbs, you most likely see squirrels every single day, all year long. Squirrels—so what? They've always lived here, just like the birds, haven't they? Turns out, no. Our whimsical furry friends are only so populous today because of a fad over 100 years ago, according to Dr. Etienne Benson, associate professor of the history and sociology of science at the University of Pennsylvania. Squirrels in parks and cities were the cool thing. Not every town had them, but everyone wanted them, including Kansas City's own William Rockhill Nelson. Benson writes that in the mid-1800s, Boston, Philadelphia, and New Haven had spearheaded the

> **SQUIRRELS**
>
> ---
>
> **What:** Squirrels
>
> **Where:** Look out your window.
>
> **Cost:** Free, unless you buy a feeder
>
> **Pro Tip:** While it's terribly tempting to attempt a relationship with a squirrel, they prefer to live among their own kind.

Everywhere squirrels were introduced, people loved them, fed them, and made little boxes for them to live in. Kansas City was no different.

Lawrence author J.R. Hooge is so captivated by squirrels that he's written a series of books about them called Leafensong. *This is Claryn from Book Two. Drawing courtesy of J.R. Hooge*

introduction of squirrels into urban spaces to add visual interest and to connect residents with nature. By the 1920s, New York City's Central Park had about 5,000 squirrels, thanks to the park's squirrel-friendly design (read: lots of nut-bearing trees).

Benson says, "These animals were being transplanted to places where they had not evolved, and also possibly places where they would not have survived if humans hadn't built cities and filled them with trees and food so the squirrels could eat. I think it's a really interesting example of how human ideas and values end up reshaping the ecologies that we live within."

DICKEY'S JEALOUS RAGE BIRTHS UNIVERSITY BUILDING

What was he so mad about?

Separating historical fact from lore is harder in some cases than others, but the way the University of Missouri-Kansas City acquired its very first building is the stuff of legends. The building that is now Scofield Hall used to be the Dickey Mansion, home of Walter S. Dickey. And when it comes to Dickey, the lore is pretty loud. The story goes that Dickey, who made his fortune in the clay sewer pipe business, and William Rockhill Nelson, the wealthy owner of the *Kansas City Star*, were bitter rivals. Word on the street is that Dickey so disliked Nelson he would do anything he could to gall him, including purchasing a 10-acre plot in view of Nelson's front porch so that after the house was built, Nelson would have to look at Dickey's mansion first thing every morning.

Historian Chris Wolff has done a lot of digging to find the truth among the tall tales. He says the men's dislike of each other turned to full-blown hatred in the summer of 1912, after Dickey finished building his mansion. Their disagreement stemmed from the presidential election that year, a race

SCOFIELD HALL

What: Scofield Hall, on the University of Missouri–Kansas City campus, was the school's first building.

Where: 5000 Holmes St., Kansas City, MO 64110

Cost: Free

Pro Tip: While you're on campus, visit the roof of the student union at 5100 Cherry Street for a spectacular view of the Nelson-Atkins Museum.

The old Dickey mansion is now Scofield Hall on the University of Missouri-Kansas City campus.

between Republican candidate William Howard Taft and Democrat Woodrow Wilson. Both Nelson and Dickey were Republicans, but Nelson's buddy Theodore Roosevelt came out of retirement and ran as a third-party candidate, splitting the Republican vote and allowing Wilson to win the election. Dickey had voted for Taft.

Nelson died in 1915, leaving a fortune to establish the Nelson-Atkins Museum of Art. Around that time, Dickey really, really wanted to get into politics, but couldn't get elected—especially after a series of articles in the *Star* insisted that a vote for Dickey was no better than a vote for mob boss Tom Pendergast. Deciding his failure was the fault of his old enemy's newspaper, Dickey sunk his whole fortune into bankrupting the *Star*. He bought two rival papers, the *Post* and the *Journal*, to put the *Star* out of business. In 1930, William Volker and the Kansas City Chamber of Commerce purchased a bunch of nearby land for a university. Three years later, with Dickey dead and his estate deep in debt, Volker asked the heirs to donate the mansion to the new school; he'd take over the expensive mortgage. And that's how the university got Dickey's house.

One story says that Walter Dickey spied on Nelson through a telescope and caught Nelson looking right back at him through his own!

COOL ROCKS, BRO

Is that supposed to be . . . something?

The Three Graces fountain by Walter Wallace Rosenbauer at the University of Missouri-Kansas City was an iconic landmark for decades. The terra-cotta goddesses of charm, beauty, and creativity frolicked in a reflecting pool, two of them seeming to squirt water at the third. In the 1960s, the fountain started to fall apart, and it was removed in 1973. Campus historian Chris Wolff says he's heard that the college decided to put the Graces in storage for safekeeping until repairs could be made, but no one knows for sure. They weren't seen again.

The spot sat empty until the university commissioned a sculpture. An artist submitted a proposal that the school liked a lot, so they hired him. The proposal and the man's name have been lost to time, but his rocks have not. Hired some time in the 1970s, the artist ordered a load of rocks hauled to the location in front of Manheim Hall. A crane lifted each rock into the empty pool where the graces had reclined. After the dust settled, university leaders noted that the pile looked nothing like the proposal, but what could they do? The sculptor never revisited the nameless jumble, which remains as the crane operator left it. Were the crane operator and artist one and the same? They might as well have been.

MANHEIM HALL ROCK SCULPTURE

What: A pile of rocks

Where: Manheim Hall at University of Missouri-Kansas City, 711 E. 51st St., Kansas City, MO 64110

Cost: Free to you, but it cost the university plenty

Pro Tip: Check out the plaques on nearby porches and buildings. See if you can find one commemorating a visit by the president of Pakistan in the early 1950s.

This pile of rocks replaced the Three Graces fountain in the mid- to late 1970s.

The Three Graces fountain in the 1940s. Photo courtesy of the University of Missouri-Kansas City archives

The Three Graces fountain had been a class gift to the university back in 1938.

A MURAL THAT MUST HAVE A MAGNETIC PULL

How can two people in Kansas City have that name?

Painter Luis Quintanilla was a Spanish folk hero. As a very young man in the 1930s, the Spanish government imprisoned him for being a revolutionary. But Quintanilla's long stint in jail worked out for Kansas City mythology because he met a man there named Julián Zugazagoitia. Remember that name, if you don't already know it.

Dictator Francisco Franco wanted Quintanilla dead after his release from prison. So Quintanilla moved to the United States as part of a program for refugee artists. He did a little of this, a little of that, and painted some publicity pieces for prominent movies. While in Hollywood, he met painter Thomas Hart Benton. Benton was close friends with University of Missouri-Kansas City president Clarence Decker and used that connection to hook up Quintanilla with work as an art teacher and muralist in Kansas City. One of his first jobs was to paint six murals on the second floor of Haag (pronounced like the "Hague") Hall with the theme "Don Quixote in the modern world." Quintanilla dedicated a whole corner of the painting to fascism, even including a tiny picture of General Franco. By then,

DON QUIXOTE IN THE MODERN WORLD

What: 1940 murals painted by the grandfather of the current director of the Nelson-Atkins Museum of Art

Where: Second floor of Haag Hall, 5120 Rockhill Rd., Kansas City, MO 64110

Cost: Free

Pro Tip: Can you locate Sancho Panza? His face belongs to Carl Kurtz, then head of maintenance, and the person who prepared the walls for the murals.

Painter Luis Quintanilla sketching a character for his mural using a student as his model. Photo courtesy of University of Missouri-Kansas City archives

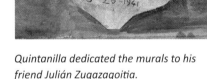

Quintanilla dedicated the murals to his friend Julián Zugazagoitia.

his old buddy from jail, Julián Zugazagoitia, had been executed by the dictator, so the artist dedicated the murals to Julián.

In a bizarre twist decades later, Zugazagoitia's grandson, also named Julián, became the director of the Nelson-Atkins Museum of Art just across the street from the university. Campus historian Chris Wolff reports that when the younger Zugazagoitia visited the murals of Haag Hall, he was quite overcome to see his own name in a dedication there on the wall.

Luis Quintanilla had lots of famous friends. Ernest Hemingway even lobbied for his early release from prison—but couldn't swing it.

HEADS OF STATE HAVE IT GOOD IN KANSAS CITY

What's so special about the president of Mexico?

Kansas City is not a hotspot for visits by foreign heads of state. To be fair, very few cities are hotspots, so we needn't despair or feel left out. The State Department's list of foreign leaders' visits to Kansas City between 1874 and 2018 includes President Rhee of Korea in 1954, President Cevdet Sunay of Turkey in 1967, and two presidents of Mexico: Ortiz Rubio in 1929 and Miguel Aleman in 1947. Of course, we know that in 1946, Winston Churchill gave a famous address at Westminster College in Fulton, Missouri, and a statue on the Country Club Plaza called *Married Love* shows Churchill and his wife sitting happily on a bench. Apart from that statue, the Mexican president appears to be the only visitor from abroad who has received any lasting attention.

Aleman must have made a big impression, but it's unclear why he decided to stop by Kansas City when he traveled to the United States to address a joint session of Congress, unless he was simply reciprocating President Truman's visit to Mexico, which had taken place just two months before. Aleman was greeted here both by President Harry Truman and by future president Dwight D. Eisenhower. Local developer J. C. Nichols

While Aleman was here, he also gave an address on the steps at the University of Missouri-Kansas City (though back then, it was just the University of Kansas City). A plaque commemorates the occasion.

This fish fountain dedicated to late Mexican President Miguel Aleman sits in front of Buca di Beppo at the Country Club Plaza.

ALEMAN COURT FISH FOUNTAIN

What: A fish fountain commemorating the Mexican president's visit

Where: 310 W. 47th St., Kansas City, MO 64112

Cost: Free, unless you sit down and order spaghetti and meatballs

Pro Tip: To learn more about other fountains, the Country Club Plaza's website offers a great map under its "hours and map" tab.

Miguel Aleman and Harry Truman in Washington, DC, in 1947. Photo courtesy of Abbie Rowe (National Archives, Wikimedia Commons)

dedicated a fish-shaped fountain to him in the alcove where Italian restaurant Buca di Beppo is now. At the time, the alcove was christened "Aleman Court."

STATUES WITHOUT LIMITATIONS

What's happening with this monument?

In 1910, when New York City's Penn Station was constructed, the *New York Times* wrote that "it was the largest building in the world ever built at one time." It covered eight acres of Manhattan and had ceilings 148 feet high: super big, super cool, and no, not here in Kansas City. Sadly, within 54 years, not that many people were riding the train, and the city decided to demolish the structure despite its glory. The architects, artists, and passengers could never have envisioned that one day a Kansas Citian would reimagine the great statuary group over the East Concourse entrance as a tribute to Eagle Scouts. But one did.

John Starr, a Kansas City businessman who was also heavily involved in scouting, heard the station was to be razed. He and his wife Martha, along with hundreds of other interested parties across the nation, wrote to the Pennsylvania Railroad president and asked for a piece of

EAGLE SCOUT MEMORIAL FOUNTAIN

What: Eagle Scout memorial that originated in New York's Penn Station

Where: The corner of Gillham Rd. and 39th St., Kansas City, MO 64109

Cost: Free

Pro Tip: You should be able to find parking on the street, but as with all street parking situations, it's best if you plan to try it at a time other than rush hour.

Another of the four Night and Day statue and clock sets is on display at the Steinberg Family Sculpture Garden at the Brooklyn Museum.

Eagle Scout Memorial Fountain at E. 39th Street and Gillham Road in Kansas City, Missouri

the action. The couple received one of four statuary sets that each included a giant laurel wreath (with a clock in the middle), two women, and two eagles. The women, crafted by Adolf Weinman, represent Night and Day (in reference to the clock they once flanked). Night is bare-breasted, which one might think twice about gifting to Boy Scouts. In place of the clock, the Starrs had an Eagle award medal installed. The entire affair went into place, along with a new fountain, in 1968.

BIRD LADY OF BROOKSIDE

Where do all these birds come from, and how do they move around?

Do you know the Bird Lady of Brookside? Sounds like she could be sort of frightening, but she's really only a statue of Hebe, the Greek goddess of youth. For the past several years, Kansas Citians have been decorating Hebe, who has stood along the Harry Wiggins Trolley Track Trail since the 1980s. They've left her all manner of bird figurines and dressed her in necklaces, bracelets, and lovely hats and wreaths. The configuration of her ornamentation frequently changes, as does the arrangement of bird offerings. Part of what makes this mystery a mystery is that interested dwellers in Brookside report that they never actually see anyone near the statue. So how did Hebe start receiving so much attention?

A team of reporters working for radio station KCUR 89.3 discovered that, for at least a little while, the giving and taking of birds was part of a geocaching game called Put a Bird on It. But were area residents already leaving offerings to the goddess before the game began? Perhaps that's how Hebe got roped in. Three years after reporting concluded, the game has been archived and no longer shows up on a map, but the goddess's festive decor and feathery friends continue to change with some regularity. Oddly, an identical statue of the goddess of youth is 10 miles away at a senior care facility in Shawnee, Kansas, with her back to the passing cars. Can you find others?

To add insult to mystery, statues of cats are now appearing alongside the birds.

Mysterious forces decorate this unmarked statue at 52nd Street and Brookside Boulevard in Kansas City, Missouri.

STATUE OF HEBE

What: Statue with mysterious embellishments

Where: 52nd St. and Brookside Blvd., Kansas City, MO 64112

Cost: Free

Pro Tip: Take a bird you can contribute to the flock.

HORSES HAVE A POWERFUL THIRST

So, fountains aren't just decorative?

Has Kansas City always been the "city of fountains"? Nay (or neigh!). It didn't gain that moniker until the 1960s. And get this: in the late 1800s, the very first fountains were not for general beautification, but for the roughly 70,000 horses that lived and worked across the budding metro. According to Sherry Piland's *Fountains of Kansas City*, horse basins went in as early as 1887, and it's easy enough to imagine old wooden troughs before that, once you're in the groove of picturing the old west. After veterinarians linked the stagnant water in troughs to the spread of a nasty equine disease, Edwin Weeks, the president of the Humane Society, designed a special trough that burbled out moving water not just for horses, but for cats, dogs, and birds as well. No one knows how many of these special animal fountains dotted the landscape before cars replaced the horses, but only one remains now, and it's fully functional at the Wyandotte County Museum.

But how did Kansas City rack up such a collection of water-involved statues? Piland suggests that George Kessler was partly, though not entirely, responsible. The German-born designer took on cosmetic urban projects in about 100 cities in numerous countries, and the Kansas City Board of Parks and Boulevard Commissioners hired him in 1892 to perk up our own

---

According to Kansas City Parks and Recreation archivist Ann McFerrin, the city maintains 48 fountains, but if you include others in the surrounding area, the number easily goes into the hundreds.

Left: The Wyandotte County Museum owns the last remaining horse water fountain in Kansas City.

Above: Kansas City horse fountain in use in 1900. Photo courtesy of Missouri Valley Special Collections, Kansas City Public Library

HORSE WATER FOUNTAIN

What: The last horse drinking fountain in Kansas City

Where: 631 N. 126th St., Bonner Springs, KS 66012

Cost: Free to see the fountain outside the front door. The museum would appreciate a donation if you walk around inside.

Pro Tip: While you're in Bonner Springs, check out the National Agricultural Center and Hall of Fame at 630 N. 126th St., Bonner Springs, KS 66012.

fair city. Kessler loved fountains. You'd think, then, that every city he helped would have as many fountains as Kansas City, but after Kessler's tenure, developer J. C. Nichols entered the scene, and he also loved the flair of a fountain. Nichols was responsible for the design of the Country Club Plaza as well as a good many of Kansas City's boulevards and shopping areas, and he agreed that fountains were the way to decorate. However, the Department of Parks and Recreation board has since removed his name from the big fountain in Mill Creek Park because of the racist policies he espoused in his lifetime.

THE BADASS CONLEY SISTERS

Can just anyone issue a curse?

Some of the bravest, smartest women who ever lived in this area were the two Conley sisters. You'd definitely never want to mess with them. First was Eliza Burton Conley, sometimes known as Lyda, the earliest woman admitted to the Kansas Bar Association. As a member of the Wyandotte Nation, though, she was also the first Native American woman admitted to the Kansas Bar. Some accounts even say that she was a member of the Missouri Bar before that. Congress authorized Secretary of the Interior James Garfield to sell what is now called the Huron Indian Cemetery for development in 1907. In fighting that, Eliza became the first Native American woman to argue a case before the Supreme Court in 1910. She wanted a permanent injunction on the sale of the cemetery, which had been a Wyandotte Nation burial place since 1843. The Conleys' parents and ancestors were buried there, and she was not about to let them be disturbed. Her case was dismissed, but in 1913 the injunction was granted after Charles Curtis, a senator from Topeka who was one-eighth Kaw, introduced an act that would permanently protect native burial grounds. Hers was the first legal battle over a sacred native burial ground. The Wyandotte County Museum reports that while the fate of the land was uncertain, the Conley sisters built a shack and took turns standing watch, guns cocked.

Lyda said: "No one shall desecrate the sacred burial ground of my ancestors. Night and day I shall guard the graves, and not a single body be moved as long as my fingers can pull a trigger."

Helena Conley's gravestone at Huron Cemetery

Lyda Conley, circa 1902. Photo courtesy of Wikimedia Commons

CONLEY SISTERS' HEADSTONES

What: Huron Cemetery

Where: 631 Minnesota Ave., Kansas City, KS 66101

Cost: Free, unless you're disrespectful during your visit

Pro Tip: Parking is slightly difficult for this stop on your adventure. Because you may find yourself parking behind a building and out of sight, don't visit the cemetery alone or in the dark.

Eliza's sister Helena was intimidating for her own reasons. First, because her birth name was "Floating Voice," and, second, because she used her headstone in the Huron Indian Cemetery to relay this message: "Cursed be the villian [sic] that molest their grave." It's possible that the misspelling nullifies the curse. Even though Helena was not a lawyer, she still did her part in protecting the land her family cherished. Helena had issued the curse while she was still alive, so by the time it appeared on her headstone it was sort of her motto. It seemed to be effective: two of President Theodore Roosevelt's sons died around the time of the curse, and he'd been ready to allow the sale of the land.

LARGEST IRON FOR MILES AROUND

Where can I go to iron this ship's sail?

Need to press a ginormous tablecloth? Like one an entire elementary school's worth of kids could picnic on together? Go on down to Central Avenue and Wilson Boulevard in Kansas City, Kansas, and check out the giant iron. The iron is close to where the Grandview Hotel, or the "Flatiron Building," stood for 100 years before the Kansas City, Kansas, city council ordered it demolished in 1987, according to a list of historical sites on Wyandotte County's website.

The big iron is a play on "flatiron," and stands as a tribute to the hotel, according to Jeffrey Jennings at the Wyandotte County Museum. A flatiron is a style of building, usually fairly tall and narrow, built to fit on a wedge of land, like this one in Kansas City, Kansas, where the roads don't come together at right angles.

GIANT IRON

What: A giant iron

Where: 1401 Central Ave., Kansas City, KS 66102

Cost: Free

Pro Tip: Just behind the giant iron is old Fire Station No. 9. It's on the National Register of Historic Places and is really beautiful.

Flatiron buildings are shaped like isosceles triangles. The architectural style was most popular in the late 1800s and early 1900s.

This giant iron is an eternal reminder of the old flatiron-shaped hotel that stood nearby.

The Grandview Hotel in 1987 just before it was razed. Photo courtesy of Wyandotte County Museum

THIS AIN'T YOUR KENNEDY CURSE

Does a president living under a curse need extra security?

On a quiet dead-end street in the Argentine neighborhood of Kansas City, Kansas, is a plaque. It's easy to miss and only tells part of a strange story. The marker is for White Feather Spring, the burial site of a man named Tenskwatawa, also known as "the Prophet." You may have heard of his older brother, Chief Tecumseh.

Tecumseh was a Shawnee intertribal leader working with the British against the United States in the War of 1812. He and future president William Henry Harrison went head to head at the Battle of the Thames; the battle did not end well for Tecumseh. His brother Tenskwatawa was so angry to lose his brother that he put a curse on Harrison (according to the Wyandotte County Museum). Tenskwatawa did not live to see the curse work; it seems to have gone into effect in the

Tenskwatawa lit his pipe and fell into a trance so deep that his family planned his funeral. When he awoke and described the visions he'd had while in the coma, his people were so impressed they called him a prophet, according to Ohio History Central.

National Register of Historic Places marker for White Feather Spring

Painting of Tenskwatawa by Charles Bird King. Photo courtesy of Ohio Historical Society (Wikimedia Commons)

years following his death. Tenskwatawa died in 1836, and President Harrison died in 1841 after only 31 days in office. Curses are hard to interpret, but curiously, every president elected in a year ending in zero from Harrison on, did not live long. It wasn't until President Ronald Reagan survived an assassination attempt that the curse was finally broken.

To wit:

- William Harrison was elected in 1840 and died in 1841.
- Abraham Lincoln was elected in 1860 and died in 1865.
- James A. Garfield was elected in 1880 and died in 1881.
- William McKinley was elected in both 1896 and 1900 and died in 1901.
- Warren G. Harding was elected in 1920 and died in 1923.
- Franklin D. Roosevelt was elected in several years, but 1940 was one of them, and he died in 1945.
- John F. Kennedy was elected in 1960 and died in 1963.

FORGET POTHOLES— THIS STREET WILL REALLY WRECK YOUR TIRES

Wouldn't it have been rough to get home with the groceries?

Street stairs—or street steps—are just what they sound like: a staircase in place of a street. San Francisco has a few, and guess what? Kansas City has one too. Visit the intersection of 13th and Ruby in the Argentine neighborhood of Kansas City, Kansas, and you'll see a long, wide, 169-step staircase that seems to lead nowhere. Former Wyandotte County resident Pat Gray said the steps were built in 1913.

Nowadays, a sign tells visitors the steps are not safe for pedestrians, but in days of yore, it was really the only road up the hill. According to the Kansas Explorers Club, after this neighborhood was constructed on a steep hill—so steep that driving up the actual road that's there now, you feel like your gears are going to start slipping—those who lived "upstairs" had no other way to access the street below or their neighbors.

Not only is this the only stair street in Kansas City, it's the only one in the state of Kansas, if the Kansas Explorers Club is correct.

STAIR STREET

What: A staircase that doubles as a street

Where: 13th and Ruby in the Argentine neighborhood, Kansas City, KS

Cost: Free

Pro Tip: This is another site that's in a neighborhood. Please respect the neighbors and the sign telling you not to walk on the steps.

A rare staircase that once functioned as the only connection between two streets

SWINGS JUST AREN'T ENOUGH FOR SOME KIDS

Mother, what's become of my cannon?

A cannon seems like a funny feature for a playground, but it's kind of a tradition at Shawnee Park in the Armourdale neighborhood of Kansas City, Kansas. Don't fool yourself imagining that you wouldn't be startled to see an army-green 155 mm World War II howitzer staring back at you as you jump off a swing. You would. But what's more startling is that this is the park's second cannon. The first, from the Spanish-American War, was donated by Congressman Joseph Taggart in March 1914. At that time, the *Globe* newspaper noted that a club called Ladies of the Grand Army of the Republic also planned to donate a flagpole for placement next to the cannon.

But for a spell during World War II, the park had no cannon. The children wept and mothers begged the department of parks

---

A HOWITZER

What: Cannon in a park

Where: S. Seventh St. (between Shawnee Ave. and Osage Ave.), Kansas City, KS 66105

Cost: Free

Pro Tip: This isn't the shadiest of parks. Try going on a cool day.

Park Commissioner William Martin placed the original artillery piece in Shawnee Park himself. Even at the time, he knew kids would play around it.

This vintage howitzer sits in Armourdale's Shawnee Park.

and recreation to give them a new one (probably). The government had taken their familiar old hunk of solid iron and salvaged it during the "steel production crisis of 1942," so says the sign on the current cannon. Lucky for the families of the community, around 1947, the Wyandotte County Salvage Committee decided it would be best to replace the missing cannon and procured today's howitzer.

THE PYRAMIDS OF PUMP STATION #39

Are those for stunts?

What's great about the pyramids of Pump Station #39 in Kansas City, Kansas, are the conversations and flights of fancy they have inspired. Owned by the Board of Public Utilities and surrounded by a barbed-wire fence, the enormous circular tank is topped by 52 pyramids. Though a sign on the fence identifies the property as a Municipal Water Lift Station, locals have spent their lives speculating about the meaning of the structure. On Facebook, several zealous commenters, former skateboarders, say as teens they referred to the pyramids as "the tits." They spent their evenings skateboarding on the concrete peaks—one person claims that the epic rideability of the makeshift arena even made it into the storied *Thrasher* magazine. But lo, at some time in the late 1980s or early 1990s, the barbed wire went up.

No one at the Board of Public Utilities would respond to requests for specific information about the unusual nature of the reservoir's cover. The signage and the barbed wire rule out the possibility that the pyramids are meant to amuse local youth, though the lack of any official statement and the unusual nature of the facility invite further guessing. Two small brick buildings stand on the property, as does an immense aboveground circular tank with a domed top. However, near the circular pyramid-topped structure is an apparently abandoned

---

PUMP STATION #39

What: A giant circle made up of 52 pyramids

Where: Lawrence Ave. and S. 13th St., in Kansas City, KS 66103

Cost: Free

Pro Tip: This facility is just begging for some good stories to be written about it. Let me know if you come up with one!

An aerial view of Pump Station #39's mysterious pyramid-covered tank.
Photo courtesy of Henry Kniggendorf

Cold War-era cinderblock building with broken windows and no indication of its past or present use. Some Facebook users insist that a substance other than water is stored beneath the 52 points. One Facebook poster dug deep and came up with a line from the movie *Total Recall* to explain that the tank holds "the integuments of Earth's atmospheric reactor. Without it, our atmosphere would not maintain its life-giving 78% nitrogen, 21% oxygen, and 1% other gases formula. Earth's atmosphere would essentially become that of Mars. The previous alien inhabitants created this reactor to sustain human life."

Examining the area from the street, one can see a concrete staircase that begins partway up a grassy hill and leads to the pyramids. The staircase is bisected by the barbed-wire fence.

MYSTERY OF THE ROSEDALE GARGOYLES

Had you ever noticed them?

The Rosedale World War I Memorial Arch sits high over the city on an isolated bluff called Mount Marty. In fact, it's so isolated that vandals defaced it for years without being caught; the tiny wrought-iron gargoyles are the monument's only sentinels. According to the well-kept archives of the Rosedale Development Association newsletter, the association approved an iron fence in late 1988, but after that, the newsletters say no more on the subject. The newsletters certainly don't explain the decision to include monster heads. Gary Keshner headed the restoration project in the early 1990s, and says he has no information about the heads either.

It's worth noting that the monument, designed by John LeRoy Marshall based on Paris, France's Arc de Triomphe, and

ROSEDALE WORLD WAR I MEMORIAL ARCH

What: Fabulous wrought-iron gargoyles guarding the Rosedale Memorial Arch

Where: Park Dr., Kansas City, KS 66103

Cost: Free

Pro Tip: Because this area is isolated, please don't visit it alone.

The arch was originally dedicated to local members of the 42nd Infantry Division, nicknamed the Rainbow Division because, unlike other units, members were from all across the nation.

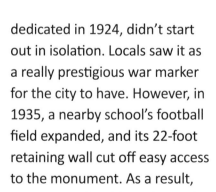
The Rosedale Memorial Arch

dedicated in 1924, didn't start out in isolation. Locals saw it as a really prestigious war marker for the city to have. However, in 1935, a nearby school's football field expanded, and its 22-foot retaining wall cut off easy access to the monument. As a result,

The Rosedale Memorial Arch is surrounded by an iron fence decorated with tiny dragon heads marked BOI 1989.

veterans and residents have alternately cared for and completely neglected the upkeep of the 34½-foot arch.

A PRISON FIT FOR A PRINCESS

Did the prisoner with the longest hair get the cell in the turret?

It's no fairy-tale world in which vagrants and petty thieves are locked away in a castle and made to sew. That life was very real for low-level female criminals in Kansas City for about 30 years— the male prisoners had public works positions. At 20th and Vine near the heart of the Jazz District, architects A. Wallace Love and James Oliver Hog designed and built a real-life castle in 1897 for the purpose of locking up ne'er-do-wells. The towers do give the impression that inmates might have been able to toss their long hair down to admirers or would-be rescuers, but it's hard to say now if that was the case. According to reporting by KCUR 89.3, "the Romanesque revival style was in vogue at the time," so it may be one of the most fairy-tale-looking prisons you've ever seen. But fairy tales don't last, and this one hasn't yet had a happy ending. The jail closed in 1924, served other purposes for 50 years, and then was abandoned.

As of this writing, the castle has no roof or doors, is filled with broken branches and glass, and bears some wild graffiti. Its future is up in the air, though every few years an enthusiastic person or group proposes a renewal project of some sort, typically with the aim of uniting the community or jazzing up the Jazz District. The city is working through a multi-million

---

The *Kansas City Star* reported in 2019 that Vewiser Dixon and UrbanAmerica will renovate the castle for office use.

The abandoned prison castle at 20th and Vine

PRISON CASTLE

What: Awesome abandoned castle

Where: 2001 Vine St., Kansas City, MO 64108

Cost: Free

Pro Tip: Don't play around in the castle; walls are crumbling, floors are falling apart, and there's a lot of broken glass.

dollar 18th & Vine Improvement Plan, which will add retail and apartment space, streetscaping, restoration of old buildings, an outdoor amphitheater, and an urban youth baseball academy among many other projects.

CHARLIE PARKER'S CHALLENGING MEMORIALIZATION

What's the big green head up to?

Charlie "Bird" Parker is one of Kansas City's most famous sons (born on the Kansas side, but he mostly grew up in Missouri). The jazz saxophonist died at only 34 and lies buried in Lincoln Cemetery. Sixty-five years later, he's still so beloved that fans gather graveside for an annual tribute, often in the form of a "21-sax salute" that typically involves more than 21 saxophones. But Parker hadn't wanted to be buried in Kansas City. His toddler daughter died on Long Island, and according to *Mental Floss*, he was adamant that he spend eternity near her. Back in Missouri, though, Parker's mother convinced his friends to bring him home, and now they're gravemates.

After that, though . . . what's the right way to say this? Somehow things kept going wrong. *Mental Floss* says that the original tombstone was off by 11 days on Parker's date of death.

His name was misspelled "Charley" in his Kansas City obituary, and an article in New York City announcing his death gave his

CHARLIE PARKER MEMORIAL

What: Big green Charlie Parker head; Charlie Parker's grave

Where: The head is outside the American Jazz Museum at 1616 E. 18th St., Kansas City, MO 64108. The headstone is at 39.0959892, −94.4809265 in Lincoln Cemetery, 8604 E. Truman Rd., Kansas City, MO 64126.

Cost: Free

Pro Tip: Visit the American Jazz Museum while you're there. Admission is $10 for adults, $9 for 65+, $6 for kids 5–12, and free for 4 and under.

Charlie Parker in New York City, 1947. Photo courtesy of Wikimedia Commons

The Charlie Parker Memorial is by the American Jazz Museum.

age as 53. Fans refused to believe he'd died of pneumonia, instead claiming he'd been punched, shot, or succumbed to liver disease (he had been a heavy drinker). In 1992, someone stole the corrected headstone. But two years later, when the second stone was finally replaced, no one had proofread it, and the etched instrument was the wrong kind of saxophone: Parker played alto, and the engraving was of a tenor sax. In the late 1990s, when Congressman Emanuel Cleaver was still Kansas City's mayor, he lobbied to move Parker's grave to a spot outside of the American Jazz Museum and create a sort of shrine. Not enough people went for the idea. In 1999, Cleaver, along with Kansas City Parks and Rec, dedicated a plaza area to Parker near the entrance of the museum instead. The big, green head there seems to blow intently on an invisible horn with "Bird Lives" carved beneath; after his death in 1955, those words showed up tagged on buildings around New York City.

In some years, entire weeks of activities are dedicated to Charlie Parker, including classes, tours, concerts, and storytelling sessions.

GOING TO KANSAS CITY

But where is 12th Street and Vine?

"Going to Kansas City" is our city's most famous song and was written in 1952 by two young men who'd never been to Kansas City. Even the Beatles covered a version of it. We know all about standing on the corner of 12th Street and Vine with our baby by our side, don't we? But wait a second—how could we? Right now, there is no true intersection of those streets, only a sign for tourists.

What you can find there now, aside from the pretend street sign, is a park in the shape of a grand piano dedicated in 2005. (Only the birds can see the shape.) The place is called the "Goin' to Kansas City Plaza at 12th Street and Vine." Parking spaces along the flat side of the park, 12th Street, are painted black and white to resemble piano keys. The Paseo and Ella Fitzgerald Lane delineate the rest of the piano. In the middle of the park is a treble clef–shaped walkway. C. J. Janovy wrote in *The Pitch* that, during the dedication ceremony, then-mayor Kay Barnes gave a key to the city to the men who wrote the song, Mike Stoller and Jerry Leiber.

> ### GOIN' TO KANSAS CITY PLAZA AT 12TH STREET AND VINE
>
> **What:** A park shaped like a piano
>
> **Where:** 1562–1500 E. 12th St., Kansas City, MO 64106
>
> **Cost:** Free
>
> **Pro Tip:** If you look at a map of the park, you'll be able to make out its baby grand shape.

12th Street and Vine only existed as a real location until the 1960s—for about 20 years after the song was written—and then was razed as part of an urban renewal project.

This park features a raised piano-shaped platform for a planter, parking spaces painted to resemble piano keys, and a decorative sign for the intersection of 12th Street and Vine.

WALT DISNEY DIDN'T INVENT MICKEY MOUSE

Just how many origin stories does Mickey have?

Our town has its own bunch of legends Kansas Citians love to tell and retell: the legend of Ernest Hemingway beginning his career at the *Kansas City Star*, for instance; the legend of basketball's humble beginnings just up the road in Lawrence, Kansas; any story you can think of related to barbecue; and Walt Disney, in general. He might be the biggest Kansas City legend of them all. After post-war stints at a couple of ad agencies, Walt decided to take a stab at his own animation studio, Laugh-O-Gram Studio, in 1922. That's not weird. That's fine, and maybe you already knew that.

But, get this: Walt didn't invent Mickey Mouse. That's according to New Jersey–based author Jeff Ryan's book *A Mouse Divided: How Ub Iwerks Became Forgotten . . . and Walt Disney Became Uncle Walt*. One of the things that Ryan pieced together through extensive research was that Walt's original partner, a man named Ub Iwerks (oob eye-werks), originally drew Mickey Mouse.

When the two animators went their separate ways in the early 1930s, and people would ask Walt to tell about Mickey's origins, his story changed nearly every time he told it; Ryan counts five stories in all. "First he invented it on the train going to Los Angeles. Then his wife helped. . . . The story just got

ThankYouWaltDisney.org is a website dedicated to converting the old Laugh-O-Gram building into a Disney museum, office space, and studio. Check it out for updates.

The site of Walt Disney's Laugh-O-Gram Studios

Mickey Mouse drawing with Ub Iwerks's name as artist. January 1, 1928. Photo courtesy of Wikimedia Commons

LAUGH-O-GRAM STUDIOS

What: Walt Disney's first studio space

Where: 1127 E. 31st St., Kansas City, MO 64109

Cost: The museum is pretty far from open. It's free to drive by the still-defunct building, but eventually, it'll be a place to visit that will most likely charge admission.

Pro Tip: The old building is under renovation. Owners say a museum is in the works.

bigger and bigger," Ryan said on KCUR 89.3's Central Standard. Walt claimed—at least once—that one mouse in his studio was bolder than the others when he fed them, so he bought a cage and kept that one on his desk. People liked that story, as well as the other stories he told, and that's how the world forgot Ub Iwerks, and Disney took credit for inventing the mouse.

WEALTHIEST BLACK GIRL IN THE NATION

Will you keep your hands to yourself, please?

A grand old boarded-up mansion in Kansas City, Missouri, once housed a girl billed as "the richest Black girl in America." By all accounts, she might as well have been assigned this title by a carnival barker, the way they attach superlatives to any extraordinary attribute a person might possess: the fattest man in the world, the tallest baby in the world, the hairiest woman in the world, and so on. The crudeness of it didn't make it untrue, though. Some histories even insist that the little girl, Sarah Rector, was the first Black millionaire in the United States, though that is debatable.

Rector was born in 1902 in Oklahoma. She was both Black and a member of the Creek (or Muscogee) Indian Nation. Creek tribal members had enslaved her ancestors, according to an article on the Kansas City Public Library website, but after the Civil War, the US government declared her family free and *members* of the Creek Nation rather than its subjects. The government gave all such descendants who were born before March 4, 1906, according to historian Tonya Bolden, acreage as part of the Dawes Allotment Act of 1887. Sarah received 160 rocky, dry, seemingly worthless Oklahoma acres valued at a total of $556.50. Her guardian agreed to lease the land to a man drilling for oil, and lo, in 1913, he hit a gusher—her land

The Kansas City Public Library reports that after Sarah moved to Kansas City, she hosted parties for celebrities, including Duke Ellington, Count Basie, Joe Louis, and Jack Johnson.

Sarah Rector's Kansas City mansion

Sarah Rector in 1912. Photo courtesy of Wikimedia Commons

THE RECTOR MANSION

What: One-time home of the wealthiest Black girl in the country

Where: 2000 E. 12th St., Kansas City, MO 64127

Cost: Free

Pro Tip: As with many of these stories, the text here only gives you the smallest idea of what the bigger story is about. It's very easy to find more information about Sarah Rector, and I hope you will.

began producing 105,000 gallons of oil a day! Sarah, being a minor, a minority, and female, worked with a white, male guardian who managed her money until 1920 when she turned 18 years old, by which point her estate was worth $1 million, and she'd settled in Kansas City.

ARTHUR KRAFT, FOREVER

Have you heard of Arthur Kraft?

If you've tooled around town enough, you've most likely at least seen his work, such as the three playful bronze penguins on the Country Club Plaza or the mural in the lobby of the Westport location of Bank of America. It's also totally likely he's standing right behind you this very second—his headstone in Calvary Cemetery on Troost Avenue threatens as much.

The artist started selling his work at the Plaza Art Fair at 13 years old in the 1930s, had a solo exhibition at a Paris museum about a decade later, and showed alongside greats such as Georgia O'Keeffe in the 1940s, according to journalist Julie Denesha. Some Kansas Citians Denesha spoke with insisted that Kraft should be as well remembered as another locally grown artist, Thomas Hart Benton. However, something dragged the man down (perhaps the difficulty of being gay during that time in history, his lack of a manager, or his battle with addiction), and by the 1950s, his spending and extravagant gifting habits also hampered his work—he'd give away even elaborate stained glass pieces for nothing. In fact, he gifted 13 stained glass panels to Overland Park Christian Church. That was one

ARTHUR KRAFT'S GRAVE

What: Arthur Kraft's work and final resting place

Where: The stained glass windows are at 7600 W. 75th St., Overland Park, KS 66204. The headstone is at 39.0042725, −94.5711136 in Calvary Cemetery, 6901 Troost Ave., Kansas City, MO 64131.

Cost: Free

Pro Tip: The headstone is flat, so in order to find it, it's easiest to look for William and Ida Sork's headstone nearby, right next to a cedar. Search Wonderful World of Arthur Kraft for more to visit.

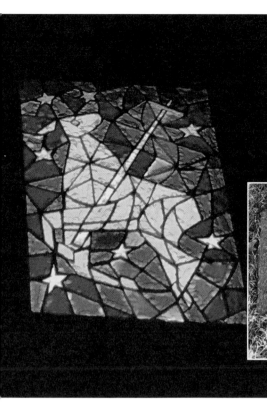

This piece called "Christ Window: the lamb with banner and seven stars" is one of 13 panels at Overland Park Christian Church at 7600 W. 75th St. in Overland Park.

Arthur Kraft's headstone in Calvary Cemetery

for Jesus and each disciple. In the early 1970s, Kraft checked into a state hospital in St. Joseph, Missouri, for alcoholism. He died in 1977, but not before deciding on his eternal, oddly punctuated, words: "Goodbye for now, I'll be back that is, if I am not already." Seems that even if things weren't going great, he still wished to stick around.

Kraft's work is on permanent display at the Albrecht-Kemper Museum of Art and Glore Psychiatric Museum, and the Nelson-Atkins Museum of Art owns, but is not currently displaying, a painting.

NO ONE WANTS TO BURN BRIDGES

Where are you hoping to go?

What makes some bridges engineering marvels and others just kind of . . . odd? Perhaps it's what they're built over, like the lovely Sydney Harbor Bridge. Perhaps it's what they connect, the way the Brooklyn Bridge joins Manhattan and Brooklyn. Maybe it's all about the flourishes like those of London's Tower Bridge, or even the length—a record held by the 102-mile Danyang–Kunshan Grand Bridge in China. The majority of bridges, as we know from everyday experience, are no-nonsense, nothing fussy; they just take us where we need to go.

But have you noticed the bridge alongside I-70 between Benton Boulevard and Indiana Avenue? You may not have because you can't drive on it. That funny little stretch of bridge links one patch of grass to another patch of grass—and not for something noble like keeping deer from getting hit by highway traffic. According to Robert Cronkleton's research for the *Kansas City Star*, the bridge acted as an on-ramp from Benton to I-70 for a while in the 1960s.

BRIDGE BETWEEN NOTHING AND NOTHING

What: A mysterious bridge that doesn't seem to connect anything

Where: I-70 between Benton Blvd. and Indiana Ave.

Cost: Free

Pro Tip: The city planned to include the bridge in a new freeway it didn't actually build, so in the 1970s, planners closed and cleared away the ramp, leaving the bridge behind.

The Bridge to Nowhere in 1964. Photo courtesy of Missouri Valley Special Collections, Kansas City Public Library, Kansas City, Missouri

Cronkleton's reporting also uncovered a way that this mystery bridge is proving useful. He found that the University of Missouri has recently completed a study about the effects of weather on a bridge that is never treated in icy weather. As of this writing, the study isn't available. However, as anyone in the Midwest can attest, highway snow management is big business, as is repairing damaged bridges. According to reporting by KCUR 89.3, the snow removal budget of Kansas City proper in 2019 was $2.75 million. That's to clear 6,400 lane miles with 200 plows. In 2018, $232 million of the Missouri Department of Transportation's budget went to road repair. Maybe the bridge study will point to a new, less costly type of road clearing and maintenance!

PRESIDENT TRUMAN WAS PRETTY HARD TO FOLLOW

You're saying there was no President Dewey?

Kansas Citians like their President Harry S. Truman stories. One particular legend, though—maybe the most famous story—is a little hard to pin down. Where exactly was Truman when he held the erroneous November 3, 1948, copy of the *Chicago Tribune* that declared "Dewey Defeats Truman"?

This book's cousin *Secret St. Louis* states that the photographer caught him at St. Louis's Union Station. The *Chicago Tribune* itself agrees, as do history.com and *Life* magazine. In fact, W. Eugene Smith's famous photograph simply looks like it was taken in a rail station. But many around Kansas City will argue that Truman was either at the Elms Hotel in Excelsior Springs or staying at Kansas City's Muehlebach Hotel.

A writer for *Politico* writes: "The next morning, the president returned to Kansas City, where he was photographed displaying an early edition of the *Chicago Tribune* proclaiming: 'Dewey Defeats Truman.'" The writer cites David McCullough's biography of Truman, but upon inspection of that book, it's clear that McCullough wrote no such thing.

The confusion seems to stem from Truman's manic travel schedule. He was at the Elms on the first of November, then at the Muehlebach in Kansas City by the morning of the second, and returned to the Elms to sleep on the evening of the second

Truman and his staff used Kansas City's Muehlebach Hotel so often that many called it "White House West."

President Harry Truman with the famous false headline. Photo courtesy of Truman Library (Wikimedia Commons)

before returning to Kansas City on the morning of the third. By the fourth, the day of the famous photograph, he was on his way from Missouri to Washington, DC, when the train stopped in St. Louis, and the photographer captured the moment Truman finally held up the copy of the paper with the false headline printed the day before.

HARRY S. TRUMAN LIBRARY AND MUSEUM

What: Dewey Defeats Truman photo

Where: 500 W. US Highway 24, Independence, MO 64050. Also visit the Excelsior Springs Visitor Center at 201 E. Broadway Ave., Excelsior Springs, MO 64024 to learn more.

Cost: Admission to the presidential library is $8 for adults, $7 for 65+, $3 for ages 6-15, and free for 5 and under. The Excelsior Springs visitor center is free.

Pro Tip: The photo printed here is not the one in the railroad station; that photo is not public domain, so you'll have to do a search if you'd like to see it.

NO, NOT THAT IHOP

Will you order pancakes when the world ends?

Most people have been to an IHOP, or at least seen the big blue roof of an International House of Pancakes from the road. But what about IHOP? You know, the International House of Prayer? (Isn't that confusing?) The pancake people filed, then dropped, a lawsuit against the prayer people in 2010 for illegal use of their acronym. Mike Bickle founded the praying IHOP in 1999 in Kansas City, Missouri, based on ideas about the end times. Members who've left say the church discouraged them from pursuing higher education because of this tight focus. (The end is coming, so why bother?) However, church leaders don't want their people learning nothing at all, so they offer a music academy, a media institute, Chinese classes, and unaccredited university hours. Bickle is cultivating a group of people he calls "forerunners," or according to a 2008 conference PDF on the church website, "messengers," to help people make sense of the end times.

INTERNATIONAL HOUSE OF PRAYER

What: International House of Prayer Church, prayer room, coffee shop, and a real estate agency to aid newcomers

Where: Global Prayer Room at 3535 E. Red Bridge Rd., Kansas City, MO 64137; Forerunner Church at 12444 Grandview Rd., Grandview, MO 64030

Cost: Free

Pro Tip: Stop in the coffee place in the IHOP strip.

The website states that college accreditation is "more of a hindrance than a help in accomplishing the purposes for which God has called us into being."

The International House of Prayer sign

Bickle writes that in 1983, he received a divine message that once he'd established 24/7 prayer, God would connect the church to "millions of Asians and their leadership in a powerful way. [God] said this would happen when we received the property that President Harry Truman once owned in Grandview (we received 125 acres of his land as a gift in 2008)." Bickle did establish 24/7 prayer in the church's prayer room where, around the clock, worshippers pray and play music, and Truman once owned the acreage.

HEY, THAT BUFFALO MANTELPIECE BELONGS TO ME!

Are Western-style and American-Georgian compatible?

When Missouri's own Harry S. Truman took office in 1945, the White House was in sad shape. In a letter to wife Bess, still in Missouri, Truman joked that the place was haunted: "The floors pop and the drapes move back and forth. I can just imagine old Andy and Teddy having an argument over Franklin." It was time for some reconstruction, which took place from 1948 to 1952. But speaking of Teddy, in 1902 he'd commissioned a very cool carved stone buffalo head mantel for the house at 1600 Pennsylvania Avenue. However, according to a *Mental Floss* article, the rustic, Western-vibe piece didn't fit the new "American-Georgian aesthetic of the reconstruction," and the mantel sort of disappeared.

TRUMAN MANTELPIECE

What: Buffalo mantelpiece

Where: 500 W. US Highway 24, Independence, MO 64050

Cost: $8 for adults; $7 for ages 65+; $3 for ages 6-15; free for 5 and under

Pro Tip: This is definitely a place to call ahead; extensive remodeling has been underway for a long time, and you want to make sure the exhibitions you're interested in will be available.

Some people thought the mantelpiece had been thrown out, but official records show it had been put in storage. Later someone discovered Truman had shipped it to Independence.

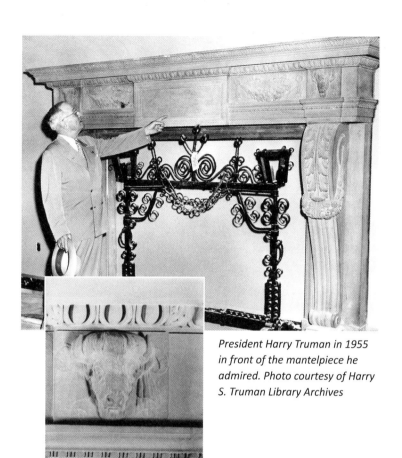

President Harry Truman in 1955 in front of the mantelpiece he admired. Photo courtesy of Harry S. Truman Library Archives

Detail work of the mantelpiece. Photo courtesy of Cecil Schrepfer at the Harry S. Truman Library

But, guess who liked it a lot? When John F. Kennedy took office a decade after the Trumans moved out, Jackie Kennedy decided another decor update was in order. And what did she want? The cool buffalo mantel. Legend has it that she wrote to Harry and asked him to return it. And he said no. The Truman Library says no such feisty exchange happened, but the story is out there. At any rate, Jackie had a replica made, which is what's in the White House now over the State Dining Room fireplace. The real one is still in Independence.

AN ENGLISH COW . . . WITH A PAST

But what kind of name is "Anxiety"?

For his name alone, this cow should be famous. But "Anxiety IV 9904" is also famous for his role as forefather of 99% of American Herefords. He's a cow with a great bio, too. Sara Gugelmeyer writes that he's "a sire whose powerful hindquarters changed the beef industry forever." Skip this sentence if you're a vegetarian: it's likely you've partaken of Anxiety's bloodline. To set the scene, it was the Midwest after the Civil War, and everyone in the cattle industry was out to breed a cow that tasted better than any other. Lots of people tried to create a mixed breed that would have the best meat for the perfect steak. Two men, Charles Gudgell and Thomas Alexander Simpson, who ran the Gudgell Simpson Farm in Independence, Missouri, would stop at nothing to find this perfect steak-bull. They traveled to England, saw Anxiety IV's spectacular hindquarters, and bought him, though according to the story, the owner said Anxiety wasn't good enough for siring, that is, making babies. Now a marker in the Golden Acres subdivision in Independence, an appropriately English-looking area, commemorates the cornerstone bull and his buyers.

According to the Cattle Site, a reference and news source for the cattle industry, more than 5 million Herefords populate 50

ANXIETY IV MARKER

What: A marker about a cow OR a delicious steak at a restaurant

Where: 1717 S. Lake Dr., Independence, MO 64055

Cost: Visiting the marker is free; the cost of the steak depends on where you go.

Pro Tip: This neighborhood really is lovely: do take a spin through it.

Anxiety the 4th's forefather, Anxiety the 3rd, in 1887. Rendering by James Harvey Sanders (Wikimedia Commons)

ANXIETY 4th

This was the site of the headquarters farm of Gudgell & Simpson, early day Hereford cattle breeders. In 1881 this firm imported from England Anxiety 4th, cornerstone sire, from which almost all Hereford cattle in America are descended. Here in a small barn on the site of the Golden Acres Clubhouse was born on Oct. 5, 1890, Beau Brummel, the most famous grandson of Anxiety 4th. Charles Gudgell's method of closebreeding of cattle resulted in the outstanding development of this strain of Herefords and gained wide fame for the firm. Gudgell was the first elected Secretary-Treasurer of the American Hereford Association.

Marker to Anxiety the 4th at the Golden Acres Clubhouse in Independence, Missouri

countries, dominating ranches "from the prairies to the pampas and from the Russian steppes to the South American veldt." If that's not cowboy poetry, I don't know what is.

The first Anxiety was so-named because his owner, a Mr. Carwardine, felt extremely anxious about his birth. Anxiety's mother, was an "expensive grand show heifer," and so fat that Carwardine wondered if either animal would survive.

COME A LITTLE BIT CLOSER TO KC; IT'S BETTER HERE

Your whole plan depended on one boat stop?

Once upon a time, an unusually intense man named William Gilpin predicted that the region around Kansas City would be the world's next major metropolitan area, like Paris or New York City. And he called this grand place Centropolis. In his book, *Mission of the North American People*, first published in 1860, he wrote: "Kansas City has the start, the geographical position, and the existing elements with which any rival will contend in vain." He called the city a "key-point of centrality and radiance, and of unrivalled excellence." But his high estimation of our humble town did not come from God as it had for the Mormons (discussed later) and the founder of the International House of Prayer. No, Gilpin depicted himself as a man of science. He had a theory about what he had identified as an "axis of intensity" along a "narrow belt or zodiac" defined by "isothermal science." In other words, we're situated along a latitude that can expect temperatures good for agriculture and human comfort. In the 1840s, he'd tested his ideas by moving to what is now Sugar Creek, Missouri, and convinced other movers and shakers to buy a bunch of land from the government. Historian Audrey Elder

---

A post office on Truman Road in zip code 64126 is marked as Centropolis Station. Also, an apartment building called Centropolis on Grand recently opened where the Grand Centropolis Hotel stood in 1880.

The historic marker for Gilpin Town Hall Trail Head is in front of the Mallinson Vineyard and Hall.

says Gilpin told the other men: "This is a geographic location that is going to create prosperity that no one has ever seen before." In 1851, a flood changed the course of the river that was part of his master plan for maximal traffic. No one would ever again stroll into town from Wayne Landing, which Gilpin had banked on. The furious investors filed suit against him to get their money back. By then, though, Gilpin had moved to Denver, which also lies along his axis and allowed him some quiet time to write his book.

Today, history enthusiast Matt Mallinson owns what may be the last verifiable bit of Gilpin's property, where he runs a beautiful winery and event space.

WILLIAM GILPIN HISTORIC MARKER AND WINERY

What: A national parks historic marker about Gilpin and a winery

Where: 3029 N. River Blvd., Sugar Creek, MO 64050

Cost: Free to stop by and see the sign

Pro Tip: Call ahead and make sure you'll be able to visit Mallinson's Winery while you're checking out the marker.

FINALLY, A CURE FOR EVERYTHING

What are you in for?

Excelsior Springs, Missouri, was billed as "Missouri's National Health Resort" after the discovery of its "healing" waters in 1880 up until 1963. In that year, federal legislation passed to prohibit the various clinics from advertising that the water could cure specific ailments—which was exactly what practitioners in the town had been doing all along. Current signage at the town's Hall of Waters notes that the clinics claimed the ability to fix pretty much anything that might ail a person, including "genito-urinary complications" and "impure or impoverished blood." Or maybe you only have arthritis. Sit in this tub of mineral water!

"Oh no, you don't," said the feds. And the town's economy went down the drain.

It's said that, in the beginning, a man who hoped to cure his daughter's tuberculosis gave her some spring water and her health quickly improved. Another story says a Civil War veteran poured spring water over a wound that had never healed, and boom: healed. So how could anyone who heard those stories resist trying it themselves and then spreading the word? Eventually, the people of the town discovered 10 main springs and five kinds of mineral water, more than anywhere in the world except for possibly Baden-Baden, Germany. By 1935, Excelsior Springs had become a resort town, and travelers

A sign in the ladies' bathing area says water choices included iron-manganese, calcium bicarbonate, sulpho-saline, and soda water.

The Excelsior Springs Hall of Waters

came from all parts of the United States and the world for healing. The city decided to err on the side of efficiency and direct all the water to one location, the Hall of Waters. In 1937, the $1 million art deco building opened. Now the Hall of Waters houses the city's visitor center but looks much the same as it did in the 1930s, including the ladies' bathing area and the water bar down the center of the lobby.

EXCELSIOR SPRINGS

What: Hall of Waters

Where: 201 E. Broadway Ave., Excelsior Springs, MO 64024

Cost: Free

Pro Tip: Plan to walk around the historic downtown—it's really lovely and the restaurants are great.

I LOVE YOU LOCKS

Who's got the key to this thing?

When saying "I love you" isn't enough, consider fastening a padlock to a bridge and tossing away the key (in a designated repository). According to *Missouri Life* magazine, a Kansas City Parks and Rec employee got the idea from the Pont des Arts in Paris and, in 2013, fixed one lock to the Old Red Bridge for her fiancé and another for her dog. About 4,000 lovers have followed suit on the now pedestrian-only bridge in William Minor Park. In case the act of clamping down the lock isn't enough, the parks department website suggests personalizing the padlock for good measure.

Regardless of whether the lock you add is for your dog, your mom, a neighbor, or an actual lover, under no circumstances should you "throw away the key." The parks department says that so many people threw their keys into the water that they became a threat to the wildlife. Instead, leave your key in the designated box. Alternately, make some art of your own with the key, like putting it on a chain for a necklace. (Or you can skip this part and just get a lock with a combo, but that doesn't really say "forever" the way a keyed lock does.)

RED BRIDGE LOVE LOCKS

What: A bridge for lovers covered in padlocks

Where: East Red Bridge Rd., Minor Park North Entrance, Kansas City, MO 64131

Cost: As much as you want to spend on a lock

Pro Tip: For similar fun, visit the Town of Kansas Observation Deck near the City Market at 1st St. and Main St. in Kansas City, MO 64105.

The city plans to make a butterfly with the keys people put in the boxes at each end of the bridge.

Minor Park invites lovers of all kinds to clamp a padlock to the bridge in honor of their affection.

EXCHANGE STUDENTS ON THE RANGE

Where do the deer and the antelope play?

If given a list of exotic animals versus domestic animals, could you sort them? Sure, you might say that a penguin is exotic in the United States. Camels are too. But how would you classify a buffalo? In his own backyard, the bison is on the fence. At Jackson County's Fleming Park, you can visit native animals in a 110-acre enclosure. The bison, elk, and white-tailed deer who used to freely roam the plains are now visible to the public at the Native Hoofed Animal Enclosure. The confinement is sad and a little hard to digest, but when you get into raising these animals on private ranches, it gets stranger still.

Amy and Michael Billings own and run Buffalo Ridge, a bison farm near Kingsville, Missouri. They sell the bison and their meat, which they say actually helps the species survive because it creates a demand for them, which, in turn, generates more money to care for the animals and increase their numbers. However, when the Billingses take the animals to slaughter, they pay higher fees to the facility than cattle ranchers do because, Amy Billings says, "Right now, bison are considered exotic—which is the ironic piece because they're actually native and cattle are exotic—but cattle are considered domestic livestock so they're treated in a different way than exotics are." In any case, while you're actually visiting the enclosure, the animals come

Many signs warn not to feed the animals any kind of grain. However, the elk seem pretty happy to accept gifts of carrots from visitors.

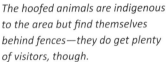

The hoofed animals are indigenous to the area but find themselves behind fences—they do get plenty of visitors, though.

so close to the fence that you'll seldom hear a discouraging word about them or the experience of getting such a good look.

NATIVE HOOFED ANIMAL ENCLOSURE

What: Native animals in an enclosure

Where: 6010 East Park Rd., Lee's Summit, MO 64064, near Lake Jacomo in Fleming Park

Cost: Free

Pro Tip: The enclosure is fairly close to downtown Lee's Summit, which has a beautiful downtown with many fabulous restaurants to choose from.

PENGUINS AND ELEPHANTS LIVE IN HARMONY

How many animal selfies can you collect?

Ever seen an Emperor penguin out in the wild? Take a trip to the Northland, and you'll find that they look much bigger in person than on the National Geographic channel. In fact, the one you'll find at Penguin Park is 25 feet tall. You'll also find an elephant, a giraffe, and a mama kangaroo—perhaps the only times you'll ever see these friends all in one spot.

Long, long ago in the 1950s, parks were for swings, tall metal slides, and dangerous contraptions such as merry-go-rounds. They were not the places of today with soft, spongy mats for kids to fall on, and colorful, safe structures for climbing. In Kansas City, they changed forever when Vernon Jones began building giant creatures, first for a place called Santa's Wonderland, and then for what became Penguin Park. According to radio station KCUR 89.3, Jones was working for Kansas City Parks and Recreation in the 1950s

PENGUIN PARK

What: A park with giant animal friends

Where: 4124 NE Vivion Rd., Kansas City, MO 64119

Cost: Free

Pro Tip: It's fun to visit with a child companion, but adults can swing and slide on their own too.

Over the years, the animals of Penguin Park have been well cared for and are within modern safety regulations.

Large animal sculptures at Penguin Park

when the city asked him to create a big Santa Claus for a winter-themed park. In those days, he couldn't just go out and buy what he wanted, so he sculpted the Santa with pipes, fiberglass, wood, plastic, and whatever else he could find. The park was a hit, so the city asked him to create some more creatures in the mid-1960s.

GEORGE PARK, THE MAN WITH NINE LIVES

How would you have used your second chance?

Park University and Parkville, Missouri, are just about as idyllic as it gets. The college's beautiful old limestone buildings are perched high on a hill overlooking the curvy, glassy Missouri River. Charming stores and restaurants line downtown Parkville's main drag. But "park" has nothing to do with a green recreational space, as one might guess. The "park" in Parkville isn't a "what," but a "who." George S. Park, that's who, and after he survived a Mexican firing squad, why wouldn't he have a place of higher learning and a whole town named for him? You'd have one too.

Historian Jason Roe of the Kansas City Public Library reports that the story of the firing squad survival, though Park's daughter perpetuated it, may not be entirely true. On March 27, 1836, Park was part of the Texian [sic] Army fighting for Texan independence from Mexico. That was back when Mexico had decided to ease its immigration rules in order to populate

> **PARKVILLE AND PARK UNIVERSITY**
>
> **What:** A charming town and university named after a man who cheated death
>
> **Where:** George is buried in Walnut Grove Cemetery, 5849-5875 on Missouri Route 9, in Parkville, MO 64152.
>
> **Cost:** Free
>
> **Pro Tip:** Visit hungry. Parkville has several really excellent restaurants.

In 1836, Park left the army and moved to Jackson County, Missouri, to be a teacher.

Mackay Hall on the Park University campus

George Park. Photo courtesy of Park University Archives

a giant chunk of real estate, and hordes of Americans moved in. On that day in March, Mexican forces condemned 400 Texian soldiers, possibly including George Park, in what was later called the Goliad Massacre. The majority of the soldiers were killed, but a few escaped. In 1844, Park started the town of Parkville, as would anyone who had escaped a firing squad, and Park University (then College) opened in 1875 for the same reason.

CITY OF CAVES

Is it scary in there?

What's in a nickname? A 2017 *Kansas City Star* article suggested that Kansas City change its nickname to "City of Caves" from the current "City of Fountains." The journalist mostly seems to have been joking, and it's unlikely that a name that conjures images of troglodytes will catch on, but City of Caves *is* fitting. Mike Bell, vice president of Hunt Midwest, estimates the city has about 20 million square feet of subterranean business space. His company owns SubTropolis, the largest cave dedicated to business in the area, with 6.5 million square feet of space for industry and a whopping 55 million square feet total. The SubTropolis website says it's home to 55 companies and has more than eight miles of paved road. These are all-limestone caves where Ford, Russell Stover, and Pillsbury signed on as the first tenants in 1964. Other than an annual 5K and 10K, there's not a lot to do there; it's mostly businesses minding their own business. According to an article by Business Insider, 4,000 or more Kansas Citians work full time in one of the many caves. Special city ordinances govern the air quality, pillars, and roads of the caves.

But, if you want to go hang out in a cave, head to S. D. Strong in Parkville, a distillery that offers tours and events such as concerts and talks about fossils. The ceilings are fairly high, and as you sip your Moscow Mule, you may forget you're underground, though being subterranean is half the charm.

SubTropolis has copyrighted "The World's Largest Underground Business Complex," so don't start your own business and try to use those words.

S.D. Strong Distilling operates out of the Parkville Commercial Underground.

KANSAS CITY'S CAVE SYSTEM

What: A wild amount of underground office space

Where: SubTropolis, 8600 NE Underground Dr., Kansas City, MO 64161

Parkville Commercial Underground, 8500 NW River Park Dr., #136a, Parkville, MO 64152

Cost: Free to drive around

Pro Tip: Call ahead to make sure the place you'd like to see is open. S.D. Strong is your best bet if you'd like to hang out underground.

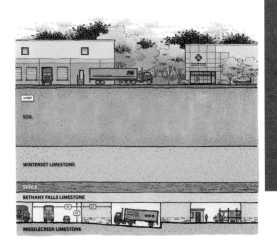

Illustrated cross section of SubTropolis (©Hunt Midwest)

TREATMENT OR TORTURE? OOPS!

Doesn't it seem like the disease is better than the cure?

Build a lunatic asylum for 250 people, and then cram in 3,000 instead. What happens? Eventually you end up with one heck of a museum. State Lunatic Asylum #2 opened in 1874 in St. Joseph, Missouri, and 250 was indeed its maximum occupancy. But after soldiers returned home from two world wars with symptoms indicative of PTSD and moral injury, and the Great Depression between those world wars had taken its toll, beds filled faster than the understaffed state-funded institution could keep pace with. The extreme overcrowding seemed to accelerate experimentation on those held in the facility. According to signage at the Glore Psychiatric Museum, doctors attempted then-popular lobotomies during this period. The museum's director of marketing and public relations, Kathy Reno, says, "We're a museum of theories that failed. Occasionally you'll see a germ of an idea, but a lot of it was terribly misguided, was not helpful."

Exhibits of sharp tools, beds equipped with straps, and short biographies of famously lobotomized patients, such as Rosemary Kennedy, tell the tale throughout the three-story building and its basement morgue. The Glore Psychiatric Museum, open since 1992, also pays homage to psychiatric

Full-sized replicas of isolation boxes and cages, a giant wooden running wheel intended to exhaust patients, various types of pools and tubs, and a mannequin poised to be burned at the stake grace the upper story of the museum.

Patient procedures once took place in rooms like this in State Lunatic Asylum #2.

treatment the world over and throughout history. Though the museum does a lot of looking back, Reno says, "Our goal for the future is how to show how far we've come. Where are we now? We've come a long way."

GLORE PSYCHIATRIC MUSEUM

What: A museum dedicated to all things psychiatric, past and present

Where: 3406 Frederick Ave., St. Joseph, MO 64506

Cost: Adults $7, seniors $6, students $5, members and children under 6 free

Pro Tip: If you're scared of clowns, stay out of the bathroom near the front desk.

FERTILE LAND THAT FIRST FED THE INSANE WENT ON TO GROW SUPERBOWL CHAMPS

Would you say that winning nourished the city's spirit?

The Kansas City Chiefs have trained at Missouri Western State University in St. Joseph, Missouri, since 2010. But long ago, that same area grew food that sustained the people of State Lunatic Asylum #2, according to Kathy Reno at the Glore Psychiatric Museum. The land held a hog farm, a 200-tree orchard, and a prize-winning dairy farm. The patients not only ate the food and drank the milk, but also worked the land. They did such a good job that one report says all that had to be bought was salt and sugar.

The state lunatic asylum opened in 1874, but in the 1860s, a "poor farm" started caring for citizens unable to care for themselves. The two overlapped, and many details of each operation have been lost to history. Reno says the hospital, in addition to using its own land, leased property in Andrew and Holt Counties, and the poor farm was on land in Andrew County at one time too.

Frances Flanagan's history of Missouri Western State University mentions an undocumented story about a choice St. Joseph citizens allegedly faced in the 1870s: would they rather

A $25 million tax credit in 2010 helped the Chiefs build an NFL regulation indoor field at Missouri Western.

The state farm in the 1960s. Photo courtesy of St. Joseph Museums

Chiefs' training camp area today. Photo courtesy of St. Joseph Museums

CHIEFS' TRAINING CAMP

What: Chiefs' training camp

Where: Missouri Western State University, 4525 Downs Dr., St. Joseph, MO 64507

Cost: Mostly $5 for admission, but check the Chiefs' website.

Pro Tip: Call ahead for availability.

have a teacher's college or a state mental institution? They chose the mental institution, and it took until 1915 before would-be students had a college, and it wasn't until 2005 that the college became a full university that offered master's degrees. All the while, the college slowly bought land that once belonged to State Lunatic Asylum #2.

BONNIE AND CLYDE DETAIL GONE AWRY IN HOLLYWOOD

You from around these parts?

Most people who have heard of Bonnie and Clyde know that theft and guns are involved with their story . . . and also that they were in love. Many imagine the story through the lens of the Faye Dunaway and Warren Beatty movie from 1967. But if someone pressed you, could you say where most of their criminal hijinks took place? In case the answer is no, here's some info: their first bank robbery was in Lawrence, Kansas, in 1932, according to *Hidden History of Kansas* by Adrian Zink. Kansas was a favorite target: maybe it had to do with the way the roads are laid out. But it was just across the state line in Missouri where the two had one of their most famous battles. The movie version of events mislabels the location. A sign in the film reads "Platte City, Iowa." Well, the real deal happened in Platte City, Missouri, now part of Kansas City.

According to WDAF-TV reporting, the felonious lovers and their accomplices checked into cabins on the grounds of the Red Crown Tavern on July 19, 1933. The party tipped their hand, though. By wearing fancy,

Platte County Historical Society marker in tribute to the lawmen who were involved in a firefight with Bonnie and Clyde in 1933

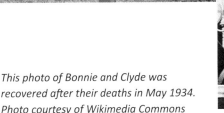

This photo of Bonnie and Clyde was recovered after their deaths in May 1934. Photo courtesy of Wikimedia Commons

expensive clothes and driving powerful cars, the locals could tell the gang wasn't from these parts and might even be up to no good. The people of Platte notified the law. Local police (and any other law enforcement they could scare up) surrounded the cabin and engaged the gang in a serious gun battle. That's the big battle in the movie, and that's where the sign appears, telling all the world (falsely) that the firefight took place in Iowa.

The couple escaped the Platte City battle, as they did time after time, but the authorities killed Clyde's brother and blinded his brother's wife in one eye.

A DOLL FOR EVERY OCCASION

These dolls aren't that scary, are they?

One can pass from childhood to adulthood in Kansas City and still somehow not know about the United Federation of Doll Clubs. It's been headquartered right under our noses since 1981, with a museum, store, annual convention, and all sorts of fascinating information about dolls—pleasant ones *and* scary ones. As staff member Donna Mills says, yes, doll collectors are well aware that a lot of people think their hobby is creepy, but that doesn't deter them. Real collectors will compete to collect the oldest dolls in the best condition from a particular artist as well as those that are simply unusual.

The museum includes thousands of donated dolls, of which about two-thirds are in storage. They're made of felt, wood, porcelain, glass, cork, goat skin, wax, nylon, wool, tin, plastic, and cellulose—anything that's ever been available to someone who wanted to create a tiny representation of a human. The oldest in the collection date back to the 1700s and weren't playthings at all, but altarpieces of saints that people smuggled out of churches when fleeing from wars, fires, and other disasters. Some dolls were made as portraits of people, such as convicted murder accomplice Countess Maria Nikolaevna O'Rourke Tarnowskaya. She didn't kill anyone personally; she just had enough lovers that it was really only a matter of time

---

Doll lovers founded the United Federation of Doll Clubs in 1949, and it now has 410 registered clubs and 8,150 individual members in 15 countries.

Countess Maria Nikolaevna O'Rourke Tarnowskaya's likeness lives in the United Federation of Doll Clubs Museum.

before in-fighting knocked off one or two of them. Other dolls in the museum acted as life-sized dining companions for kids to sit with when they weren't allowed to dine with adults. One in particular, Madeline, was a travel companion to a girl named Alice in 1868. Madeline had luggage, jewelry, boots, and a whole wardrobe; Alice's homework included keeping a diary of everything Madeline did in her world travels. All of her accouterments, and plenty else, are on display here.

UNITED FEDERATION OF DOLL CLUBS

What: Doll club world headquarters

Where: 10900 N. Pomona Ave., Kansas City, MO 64153

Cost: Adults $4, children 6–12 $2, students $1, members and children under 6 free

Pro Tip: It's tempting to take a self-guided tour, but definitely walk around with a guide if one is available.

HEART OF AMERICA, WRIT LARGE IN WOOD

Did those trees form a heart all on their own?

It took 10 years for Kansas City's living heart to grow large enough that airplane passengers could see it as they landed and took off from Kansas City International Airport. From 1990 until 2000, according to the *Kansas City Star*, volunteers from the Heart Forest Foundation spent Earth Day weekend planting trees concentrically in the shape of a heart: cedar, oak, ash, pine redbud, and hackberry. The forest appears considerably less defined today than it did at the outset, thanks to some changes in farm leasing and leadership at the Aviation Department. The *Star* reports that the foundation is discussing how to begin reshaping the image.

Two visitors to Kansas City prompted the heart project. At a meeting to mark the World Peace Celebration in Kansas City in 1987, Chief Leon Shenandoah of the Iroquois Nation said that his heart warms and his spirit soars when he's in Kansas City, according to the *Star*. Robert Muller, former assistant

HEART FOREST

What: A forest shaped like a heart

Where: North Brightwell Rd. and NW 104th St., Kansas City, MO 64153

Cost: Free to see it from an airplane (after the cost of a seat)

Pro Tip: Full disclosure: I have tried to find this from the sky and have not been able to. It really is down there, but it's going to take some dedication to spot it.

Local architect Bob Berkebile drummed up support to create this symbol for what he called "the unique KC Heart Spirit."

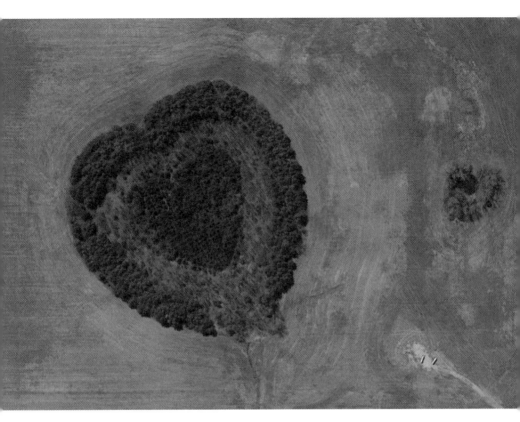

*Aerial photo of the heart forest near the Kansas City
International Airport. Photo courtesy Google Earth*

secretary-general of the United Nations, suggested that a proper
symbol of that feeling would be a giant heart-shaped forest.
AmusingPlanet.com shows a forest in England that's also shaped
like a heart, except in that case, the heart is an empty space with
trees all around it. For more information about Kansas City's heart
forest, go to creativeprocess.net/heartforest.

LIFE-SIZED CALENDAR INVENTED BY ANCIENT HUMANS

But how does it work?

Early Missourians—if you want to call them that for fun—built an amazing solar calendar in Smithville. During the Middle Mississippian period between 700 and 1000 AD, members of the Cahokian tribe created one of four known life-sized timekeepers. Three, found elsewhere around the Midwest, are circular, but the one in Smithville is square. According to information from the Smithville Lake Park Rangers station, a team of archaeologists working with the Army Corps of Engineers discovered the unusual formation in 1978. Why was a team of archaeologists hanging out in Smithville with the Army? The Army Corps of Engineers had plans to flood the area and didn't want to sink anything really interesting—at least not until the archaeologists documented it.

The Clay County Superintendent of Historic Sites said the solar calendar was way too fascinating to wash away and forget forever, so he ordered a full-sized replica built on the shore of what is now Little Platte Park. Scientists from around Kansas City and as far away as Woods Hole, Massachusetts, have studied the 36-square-foot formation trying to fully make sense of its function, but so far no one knows exactly how it worked. Forty years after the park built the replica, a new replica is replacing

There'll be 12 poles on the east, west, and north sides, double rows of five and six poles on the south side, and some in the middle.

In fall of 2020, the new version was under construction. Photo courtesy of Henry Kniggendorf

it, due to be finished by the end of 2020. Maintenance specialist Olen Reed is in charge of aligning 50 14-foot poles as closely with Polaris as possible.

WOODHENGE

What: Replica of ancient Cahokian calendar

Where: The site is near the marina at 39.4127, -94.5422 in Little Platte Park on Shelter Rd., Smithville, MO 64089.

Cost: Cash only daily entrance fee: $6 per vehicle; $20 for a vehicle and boat.

Pro Tip: This park is great for picnics, hikes, bike rides, or water sports. Go prepared!

A NICE MAMA GHOST

Am I the only one who feels that?

Pregnant women are a magnet for a lot of things, including attention from all manner of helpful strangers. No living Kansas Citian is close with Eliza Wornall, so add her to the list of concerned "strangers" who'll run to assist anyone who's expecting. The odd thing about her, though, is that she's a ghost. Sarah Bader-King, event director for the John Wornall and Alexander Majors houses, says that beginning soon after the Wornall House opened as a museum in 1974, pregnant visitors and staff felt a protective presence. Bader-King says that the house has a light fixture that can only be turned off by leaning over a banister—whenever the task falls to an expectant mother, she feels a hand steadying her.

It's fitting that the house would be haunted by Eliza rather than the scores of men who died there while it functioned as a Civil War hospital. She was wealthy landowner John Wornall's second wife and bore six children on the property over the 11 years they were married. Only one of those children survived. The Wornall House, located between what is now 59th and 67th Streets and Main and State Line, was too dangerous to inhabit in the

WORNALL HOUSE GHOST

What: Friendly ghost at the John Wornall House

Where: 6115 Wornall Rd., Kansas City, MO 64113

Cost: Adults $8, seniors and students $6, children under 12 $5, children under 5 free

Pro Tip: Visit the Shawnee Indian Mission state historic site—Eliza's father was Thomas Johnson, the man who started the mission. (The school district Shawnee Mission is named for the institution, and Johnson Drive is named for the man).

Wornall House. Photo courtesy of Wornall House Museum

Now-ghost Eliza Wornall between 1850 and 1854. Photo courtesy of Wornall House Museum

mid-1860s while the Civil War raged, so the family was living in their Westport home at the time of Eliza's death, just one week after the delivery of her seventh child, the second to survive. After the Civil War, Eliza's cousin Roma returned to the big house in 1874 as John Wornall's third bride and mother of three more children, two of whom lived. Perhaps it was in wanting to help Roma that Eliza began haunting the mansion, but who can know what's in a ghost mama's head?

John Wornall completed his big house in 1858 on 500 acres. For several years before that, the family lived in a smaller nearby structure.

A HILL THAT ISN'T A HILL

Are those relics under there?

The Kansas City metro area has its share of suburban neighborhoods, many of which are broken down into subdivisions with tantalizing names that reference hills, lakes, rivers, glens, dales, valleys, and forests. As any suburbanite can explain, even if a geographic feature is on the big concrete sign on the corner, you can't assume it's a real part of the landscape. But this is not so with the Indian Mound neighborhood.

The mound itself is a bit of a mystery. According to an article by David Remley on the neighborhood association's website, anthropologists can really only speculate about the nature of the mound: Was it used as an elevated area for signaling? Perhaps it's a mass grave. Maybe it's simply an ancient landfill. He writes that Middle Mississippians built similar mounds around St. Louis and could have been here as well circa 800 AD. This is guesswork, but Remley also references documented digs in the spot from 1877 through 1923, during which eager excavators unearthed bones, fireplaces, and tools—none of the work adhered to any scientific method, however. No one noted precise locations, depths of objects, or much else. In 1937, the Works Progress Administration halted further tampering by covering the mound with fill dirt, bringing it to the height it is today. No one has messed with it since. An article in

Builders in the area have found Native American artifacts when digging foundations. Indigenous peoples lived for hundreds of years where these Kansas Citians now live.

The Indian Mound neighborhood is so-called because of this hill.

The Indian Mound Neighborhood sign stands at the edge of a Price Chopper parking lot off of Independence Avenue. Photo courtesy of Rosemary Kniggendorf

INDIAN MOUND

What: A hill that's most likely a burial site, or at least buried bits of another culture's past

Where: Find it at Gladstone Boulevard and N. Wheeling Avenue, Kansas City, MO 64123

Cost: Free

Pro Tip: The mound isn't much to look at, but its height makes it a fun spot for a picnic.

Smithsonian Magazine suggests that early archaeologists created a narrative and mythology around the mounds of a city called Cahokia, in particular, that erased rather than preserved the work of that people. Across the Midwest and Southeast, mounds seem to be part of complex city-type layouts. Is the mound in the Indian Mound neighborhood one such hill? No one is sure!

THE TRUE TALE OF A TRUCK-EATING BRIDGE

How tall is my truck again?

Have you ever seen a man-eating chicken? How about a man eating chicken? Not much for punctuation humor? Try this on for size, and it's not a joke at all: Kansas City has a truck-eating bridge. Yes, it's true! The 12-foot high underpass has been gobbling up trucks since it was built in 1937. The truck-eating bridge, also called the US-24 overpass, is the responsibility of the Kansas City Terminal Railway, according to reporting by KCTV5.

Just like an innocent child approaching a bridge that houses a troll, unsuspecting trucks approach, speed about two feet into the dark, and are snatched up by the ferocious, fanged maw. Sometimes the trucks are completely shredded, sometimes just stuck, and, at other times, they're twisted into a U shape. Residents tell KCTV5 that this

AN UNDERPASS WITH A DANGEROUSLY LOW CLEARANCE

What: A bridge that gobbles up trucks

Where: At Wilson Road and Independence Avenue between CVS and Price Chopper

Cost: Free, unless you're driving a vehicle over 12 feet high

Pro Tip: Take a different route if you're a truck driver.

This bridge has its own Facebook page where people post photos of what happens when truck drivers don't heed the warnings. See what it's eaten this week @abridgeinmissouri.

This bridge has a clearance of 12 feet, period.

Whether a trucker sees the sign when it's too late to stop or doesn't notice the sign at all, the bridge has many ways of taking down a tall vehicle. Photo courtesy of Sherry Lynn Peck

happens at least five times a year, in spite of flashing lights and posted warnings, causing major indigestion for all involved.

Area residents post on social media about the bridge's exploits and appear to be unable to get over how, year after year, truckers simply ignore the flashing lights and the big sign that clearly says the clearance is 12 feet and ZERO inches.

HALL OF WATERS (page 56)

BIRD LADY (page 14)

INDIAN MOUND (page 82)

BIG CAT SANCTUARY (page 150)

Photo courtesy of Steve Klein

PRISON CASTLE (page 32)

HAAG HALL MURALS (page 8)

MOONLINER III (page 110)
Photo courtesy of Wikimedia Commons

FISH FOUNTAIN (page 10)

EAGLE SCOUT FOUNTAIN (page 12)

CHARLIE PARKER STATUE (page 34)

FLOCK (page 122)

PYRAMIDS OF PUMP STATION #39 (page 28)
Photo courtesy of Henry Kniggendorf

PENGUIN PARK (page 62)

OLDEST MOVIE THEATER IN THE WORLD (page 180)

SWOPE MURDERS MEMORIAL (page 136)

LOVE LOCKS (page 58)

THE ELMS (page 46)

THE BEST GHOST YOU COULD HOPE TO HANG WITH

What's funny to a ghost?

A ghost is really only a problem for people who are afraid of ghosts. So, before Stephan Zweifler's frightened friend flies in from California for a visit, Zweifler sits his ghost down for a talk. He tells her to behave and not bother the guest. Zweifler and partner Carl Markus own and live at the Inn at 425 off of Independence Avenue and have a good rapport with ghost-woman and former owner, Emeline Twiss. Zweifler doesn't hesitate to put her in her place. "But the cost for that is that she comes up to our bedroom and wakes me up. She has that kind of sense of humor. She whispers in my ear," Zweifler says.

Twiss was one of the first, if not the first, female bank presidents in the area. She was the president of the Ladies' Mutual Loan and Investment Association of Kansas City, Missouri, died in 1906 and was buried at the Elmwood Cemetery. But why tromp through a graveyard to meet this ambitious and brilliant woman? Zweifler isn't the only person Twiss talks to. At least twice now, guests have inquired over breakfast: "Who was in our room last night?"

The inn was just a regular Queen Anne-style house back in 1888 when the Twiss family lived there. Independence Avenue had some of the grandest houses and residents in Kansas City for many years.

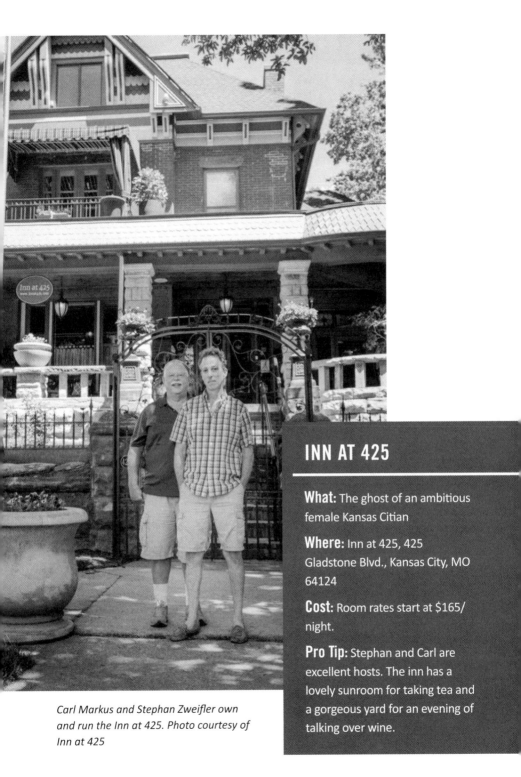

INN AT 425

What: The ghost of an ambitious female Kansas Citian

Where: Inn at 425, 425 Gladstone Blvd., Kansas City, MO 64124

Cost: Room rates start at $165/night.

Pro Tip: Stephan and Carl are excellent hosts. The inn has a lovely sunroom for taking tea and a gorgeous yard for an evening of talking over wine.

Carl Markus and Stephan Zweifler own and run the Inn at 425. Photo courtesy of Inn at 425

DEAR ABBY FOR THE DEAD

You want me to do *what*?

Do you have any advice you wish you could repeatedly offer friends, family, and strangers for all of eternity? Baseball hall of famer LeRoy "Satchel" Paige sure had a lot to say, and he wrote it down. But ink fades and paper yellows, rips, and is easily misplaced, so he had his suggestions carved into his tombstone. Topping his list of tips and tricks is "Avoid fried meats which angry up the blood." And a little further down: "Keep the juices flowing by jangling around gently as you move." You'll have to see the rest for yourself to take full advantage of them.

Paige was with the Kansas City Monarchs for 27 years—an excellent run for any professional athlete—and one can only speculate that he felt he was the right man for the job of telling others "How to Stay Young," which is the title of his six-item list.

The pitcher played in the Negro League, until he broke into the Major League on his 42nd birthday, July 7, 1948, making

LEROY "SATCHEL" PAIGE'S HEADSTONE

What: Satchel Paige's instructions from the afterlife

Where: Forest Hill Cemetery, 6901 Troost Ave., Kansas City, MO 64131

Cost: Free

Pro Tip: If you're at the baseball museum, you'd be missing out if you didn't walk across the building and also visit the American Jazz Museum.

Learn more about Satchel Paige by visiting the Negro Leagues Baseball Museum at 1616 E. 18th St., Kansas City, MO 64108.

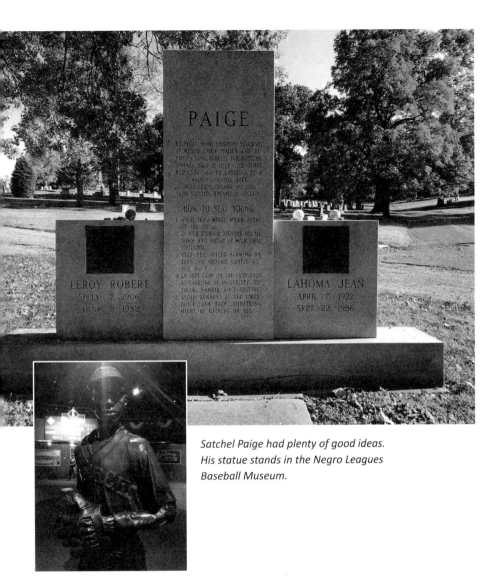

PAIGE

HE BEGAN WORK CARRYING SUITCASES
AT MOBILE UNION STATION AND DE-
VISED A SLING HARNESS FOR HUSTLING
SEVERAL BAGS AT ONCE. THE OTHER
RED CAPS SAID HE LOOKED LIKE A
"WALKING SATCHEL TREE."
THUS LEROY BECAME SATCHEL
AND SATCHEL BECAME A LEGEND

HOW TO STAY YOUNG
1 AVOID FRIED MEATS WHICH ANGRY
UP THE BLOOD
2 IF YOUR STOMACH DISPUTES YOU LIE
DOWN AND PACIFY IT WITH COOL
THOUGHTS
3 KEEP THE JUICES FLOWING BY
JANGLING AROUND GENTLY AS
YOU MOVE
4 GO VERY LIGHT ON THE VICES SUCH
AS CARRYING ON IN SOCIETY. THE
SOCIAL RAMBLE AIN'T RESTFUL
5 AVOID RUNNING AT ALL TIMES
6 DON'T LOOK BACK. SOMETHING
MIGHT BE GAINING ON YOU

LEROY ROBERT
JULY 7 1906
JUNE 8 1982

LAHOMA JEAN
APRIL 7 1922
SEPT 22 1986

Satchel Paige had plenty of good ideas.
His statue stands in the Negro Leagues
Baseball Museum.

him the oldest MLB rookie, a record which still stands according to some sources. And according to oldest.org, Paige also holds the record for the oldest player in the MLB; he pitched his last game just before he turned 60. Paige lived to be 76 and died after a heart attack, so he was also a decent advertisement for the advice he presumably lived by. And though these achievements stand, history.com reports that while records showed he was born in 1906, Paige claimed that he wasn't really sure when he was born. At one point he even offered cash to anyone who could show him the document with his date of birth.

A DIY FLIGHT SIMULATOR!

Are you in an airplane or home on your couch?

Yes, there are space and aerospace museums, aviation museums, and even flying museums (watch out!), but Kansas City has the only museum specifically devoted to airline history. And within that museum are both a flight trainer and a flight simulator. The Curtis Wright Corporation built this Richard Dehmel–designed trainer in 1953 to—you guessed it—train pilots. The simulator, on the other hand, allows visitors to fly World War I planes as well as modern airliners and fighter jets. The museum's website notes that experienced pretend-pilots can even fly a Lockheed Super G Constellation N6937C, a 1950s-era plane, which the industry and enthusiasts also called a "Connie."

Though the simulator is high-tech in many respects, it's also a do-it-yourself project. Matt Thomas founded Roger Dodger Aviation in 2005 with the idea of making flight more accessible

FLIGHT SIMULATOR

What: DIY flying simulator kit. Fly anything!

Where: The Airline History Museum is in Hangar 9 outside the Downtown Airport, 201 NW Lou Holland Dr., Kansas City, MO 64116.

Cost: General admission is $10, but discounts are available for children and active duty or retired service members.

Pro Tip: If you're prone to motion sickness, take a plastic bag with you.

Many of the materials required to build a Roger Dodger simulator are available at home improvement stores, and his DIY videos are online.

Top: A Roger Dodger Flight Simulator

Bottom: Model Shannon Walsh simulates
using a flight simulator. Photos courtesy of
Matt Thomas

to the general population. According to ATPFlightSchool.com,
learning to fly for real costs between $64 and $81 thousand, which
doesn't sound accessible at all. Thomas may be onto something!
Using his suggested methods, anyone with a computer could be
high above the clouds in no time.

THE VESSEL IS READY; NOW WE JUST NEED THE TECHNOLOGY

Say, how can I get to the moon from Kansas City?

If people travel through the air on an airliner, what do they travel to the moon in? A moonliner! Well, maybe "spaceliner" would have been a better name. In any case, Kansas City has two such rockets. According to Werner Weiss, curator of Yesterland, a website dedicated to discontinued attractions, a 72-foot high rocket called Moonliner I was a Disney landmark from 1955 to 1966. The rocket was sponsored by Trans-World Airlines and bore its logo. TWA's headquarters moved to Kansas City in 1956, and back then, the airline was so major that it expected to offer passenger service to the moon, Weiss writes. So of course TWA made a 35-foot replica of Disney's moonliner (called Moonliner II) and stuck it on top of their HQ. Just five years later, though, both rockets were looking pretty silly and no one was visiting the moon, so TWA stopped sponsoring the one at Disney and removed Moonliner II from its roof. Moonliner II had a second career for the next 30 years as the mascot of an RV park.

MOONLINERS

What: Two moonliner rockets

Where: The Airline History Museum, 201 NW Lou Holland Dr., Kansas City, MO 64116, and Barkley Advertising, 1740 Main St., Kansas City, MO 64108

Cost: Rolling by Barkley is free, but the museum charges adults $10; children 13-17, seniors, and active duty or retired military $5; and children under 13 nothing.

Pro Tip: Try to pull over before you start gawking at the moonliner on Barkley's roof—we don't want you to get rear-ended!

The Moonliner IV sits atop the Barkley Advertising building in the Crossroads Arts District.

In 1988, the totally outdated TWA building in Kansas City closed and sat defunct at 18th and Baltimore until the new millennium, when a developer restored its original 1950s glory. What do you think the developer wanted? The moonliner for the roof! Kansas Citian Dan Viets had restored Moonliner II, which is now at the Airline History Museum, and said he'd worked too hard to see his rocket sit outside and fill with birds again. He wouldn't sell. So, in 2006, developer Brad Nicholson built Moonliner IV and welded it to the roof of the newly restored building that houses Barkley Advertising.

Moonliner III, built in 1998, is at Disneyland advertising Coca-Cola.

WHILE ALL THE WORLD IS WATCHING US, LET'S MAKE MURAL HISTORY

How did you celebrate the solar eclipse?

When Japanese tourists rent a whole parking lot at Menard's in Missouri, you know something big is going down. Something so big that maybe, just maybe, Kansas Citians can figure out how to plan events around it for years to come. That's how artist Mark Allen started planning the first big mural-painting event in Kansas City during the solar eclipse of 2017. "It slowly snowballed into wanting to have events, tying in astrology and the significance of the eclipse for people," he said. He grabbed artist friends Ami Ayars and Jason Harrington, and they brainstormed and executed the painting bash they named Solanoir. They thought that while Kansas City had the eyes of the world as the best place to view the eclipse, it was a great time to draw attention to the city's exploding arts scene. In fact, they thought they'd see if they could beat out famous mural parks in Miami (Wynwood), Philadelphia, and Brooklyn (Bushwick) as the most densely painted mural park.

Twenty-six muralists created a total of 20 new murals during the week of the eclipse. Fourteen of those artists traveled from nine other states, and one came from Brazil. The artists have made the mural painting an annual festival of sorts called

All told, Kansas City has about 70 murals—more than enough reason to place the local arts scene alongside those of larger metropolitan areas.

Top: "Owl-Hooded Eclipse" by Jonathan Munden

Bottom: Untitled mural by Patrick Hershberger, @gobonussaves, and Ken Dushane III, @phybr

SpraySeeMO. In 2019, 49 artists from four countries and 14 states added 42 new murals in five parts of Kansas City. It took 4,710 cans of spray paint.

THIS COW IS ALL BULL

Can you see them way up there?

Not to be off-color or offensive—this is an all-ages book—but Kansas City is home to some of the biggest cahones you could ever imagine. Some call the owner of said cahones "Bob." Others just call him the *Hereford Bull*, the iconic 5,500-pound, 12-foot-tall bovine guardian of our fair city. He's so high up in the air (90 feet) that it's hard to see the anatomical details.

The American Hereford Association originally commissioned Bob for its then-new building at 715 Kirk Drive in Quality Hill and dedicated him in a 1953 ceremony with President Dwight D. Eisenhower in attendance. According to the Kansas City Parks website, Paul Decker designed the 19.5-foot fiberglass marvel. Bob went into storage in 1997 when the Hereford Association moved, but public outcry demanded his return to public view, according to the City of Fountains Foundation website. In 2002, he was put out to pasture in Mulkey Square Park.

HEREFORD BULL

What: Biggest anatomically correct bull you could ever hope to see

Where: Mulkey Square Park, W. 13th St. and Summit St., Kansas City, MO 64105

Cost: Free

Pro Tip: Bob is visible from I-35 near exit 2W, but if you go to the park, you can walk right up to the base of his pylon.

On October 25, 1954, Life ran a story about Bob with a series of photos, including one that clearly identifies him as male.

114

Bob the Hereford Bull is an iconic Kansas City sight, but few know he's got all of his parts. Photos courtesy of Henry Kniggendorf

THE SPOT NOT NAMED FOR LEWIS AND CLARK

Just who is this Clark?

Clark's Point is a spot at the intersection of Eighth Street and Jefferson near Quality Hill, but who is Clark? If you're standing on the windswept bluff overlooking the West Bottoms and the Kansas River, it takes no great leap of the imagination to step into the beat-up boots of Meriwether Lewis and William Clark. As the sun glinting off the river dazzles the eyes, it's June 1804 again, and the bluff appeals as a great spot for a fort. Jot that down in your journal. And look at that—an enormous sculpture of the famous expeditioners with Seaman, their trusty Newfoundland. Sacagawea, her baby, and Clark's inherited slave, York, are with them. So Clark's Point must be all about Lewis, Clark, and the gang, right? Guess again!

Historian Bill Worley says that Clark's Point was actually named after one of Boss Tom Pendergast's allies, Charles "Chuckles" Clark. Clark served on the city council for the old first ward through the 1930s, and that's the first ward down yonder, the same expanse Lewis and Clark had their eyes on.

So what's with the big Lewis and Clark statue? They really did visit that spot twice, according to city signage. The city installed Eugene Daub's statue in 2000 to coincide not with the

When Lewis and Clark visited, Clark noted seeing "Parrot queets." According to *Hidden History of Kansas*, "the Carolina parakeet was a green-plumed neotropical parrot with an orange face and a yellow head," and they lived right here.

The Kansas and Missouri Rivers run into each other in the West Bottoms.

Lewis, Clark, and the gang

LEWIS AND CLARK STATUE

What: A park on a bluff overlooking the West Bottoms

Where: W. 10th St. and Jefferson St., Kansas City, MO 64105

Cost: Free

Pro Tip: UMKC professor and novelist Michael Pritchett wrote a fictionalized account of part of Lewis and Clark's journey that really captures the imagination. Check it out: *The Melancholy Fate of Capt. Lewis.*

anniversary of Lewis and Clark's visit to the spot 196 years prior, but with the 150th birthday of Kansas City itself.

JIM PENDERGAST, THE SHUFFLED-AROUND BROTHER

Tom Pendergast had a brother?

Case Park is home to a statue of Jim Pendergast. Who is that, you ask? He's older brother to Boss Tom Pendergast who ran Kansas City from the mid-1920s to the late 1930s. Really ran it, as in controlled the police force, elected officials, the bar scene, most construction projects, and so on. But brother Jim was powerful, too, long before Tom ruled. Jim Pendergast was the old first ward's alderman. Now, his stony eyes are fixed on that great view of the West Bottoms, the part of town he started his career in, first as a saloon owner, and later as its representative and alderman.

For decades, Jim's statue, commissioned by Tom, gazed upon his ward from a vantage point in Mulkey Square, until, according to *Flatland* magazine, the construction of I-35 destroyed his spot in West Terrace Park. So the city relocated Jim to his current perch in 1990. It turns out that even the park itself, which is called Case Park, was a Tom Pendergast project, according to historian Bill Worley. Kansas Citian George Case donated

---

JIM PENDERGAST STATUE

What: Statue of Tom Pendergast's brother

Where: 905 Jefferson St., Kansas City, MO 64105

Cost: Free

Pro Tip: A building just up the hill from the Pendergast statue is the very exclusive River Club. The club's website boasts that from the living room "a man can stand and see five counties and two states and the stream of life through them."

Jim Pendergast was Boss Tom Pendergast's older brother. His statue shows him with his two children.

land for the park to the city in 1944—between Tom's release from serving 15 months at the federal penitentiary in Leavenworth and his death in 1945. The park is named for Case's father, Ermine Case.

Jim Pendergast served nine terms on city council. When he decided to quit in 1910, his little brother Tom won his seat.

THE BIRTHPLACE OF KANSAS CITY

Why is this sometimes called Cow Town?

A festival-goer wandering around Boulevardia on a summer evening might not realize she's just spilled her beer on the birthplace of Kansas City. The West Bottoms, often called the Stockyards District, used to be home to, well, the stockyards that put this cow town on the map. To look at it now, you might not be able to imagine that the nine-story Livestock Exchange Building was billed by the Stockyards Preservation Company in the 1970s as "the single most important structure that Kansas City still has to tell the story of the powerful role it played in the development of the West."

At 213,751 square feet, the structure was the largest livestock exchange building in the entire world. But why did cattle people need so much office space? Because this little 4.4-square-mile area is the fertile crescent of the Midwest. With part of it in Kansas, part of it in Missouri, and all of it nestled in the confluence of the Missouri and Kansas Rivers, the region was ideal for trade and for watering animals. At their peak, the stockyards brought in $350 million annually. That's millions and millions of cattle, mostly, but also mules, horses, and whatever other beasts people wanted to buy and sell.

Sadly, the flood of 1951 set operations on a downward trajectory that the Bottoms are only now recovering from, albeit

After a $13 million renovation, the stock exchange building is now home to dozens of tenants, including artists, entrepreneurs, and restaurants.

COPYRIGHT, 1906, BY
DETROIT PUBLISHING CO.

LIVE STOCK EXCHANGE, KANSAS CITY, MO.

Livestock Exchange Building. Photo courtesy of Wikimedia Commons

minus the mooing. The last cattle auction took place on Sept. 26, 1991. The Bottoms are now home to First Festival Weekends, four epic haunted houses every fall, and—many locals' favorite—the large-scale beer and music festival called Boulevardia, although this is subject to relocation.

LIVESTOCK EXCHANGE BUILDING

What: The birthplace of Kansas City

Where: The Livestock Exchange Building at 1600 Genessee St., Kansas City, MO 64102

Cost: Free

Pro Tip: Check out writer Karla Deel's book for more great stories about the Bottoms. It's called *Storied & Scandalous Kansas City: a History of Corruption, Mischief and a Whole Lot of Booze.*

A LOT OF TROUBLE FOR A LOW-VISIBILITY FOOTBRIDGE

Each bird is different?

This footbridge is a work of art, and I'm not just saying that because it's pretty. Installed in 2012, *Flock* by Kansas City transplant Jesse Small, is a public art installation on the north end of the trail that runs over I-670. As far as footbridges go, it's not all that grand. If you look up footbridges you'll find some wild designs that allow pedestrians to cross great expanses or put them high above breathtaking views. What's interesting about this is the detail work for a bridge that's more or less out of the way and nearly hidden. But the location does afford walkers a truly panoramic view of the West Bottoms. Seventy-two metal panels of painted black ravens flank the sine wave–shaped path of the walkway, and it's the sort of spot one only finds while out on a lunchtime run or waiting for a child to finish ball practice at nearby Mulkey Square Park. Signage quotes Small as saying: "Typically, when we see a flock of birds, they are numerous and they all look identical, but the differences might well be massive." To ensure their individuality, Small drew each bird in chalk on quarter-inch thick iron panels before he cut their outlines by hand. Each bird truly is unique—just like the bridge.

The bridge is behind the FBI building and connects Mulkey Square Park and Jarboe Park, two of the oldest parks in Kansas City, Missouri.

"Flock" displays impressive metalwork.

Since *Flock*'s installation, Small has also installed work at Arrowhead Stadium, The Jewish Community Center of Greater Kansas City, Olathe Parks and Rec, and the University of Kansas Medical Center.

FLOCK

What: Flock of completely unique metal bird cutouts on a footbridge

Where: The intersection of Westside Neighborhood Trail and Riverfront Heritage Trail, between Mulkey Square Park and Jarboe Park

Cost: Free

Pro Tip: On a day with a blue sky, the birds make an excellent backdrop for a selfie.

SNAKE SHMAKE

She eats what?

The world's longest snake living in captivity is right here in Kansas City. She's a reticulated python named Medusa owned by Full Moon Productions. Medusa was born in 2004, is over 25 feet long, and weighs at least 350 pounds. According to Fox 4 News, her favorite foods include live raccoons, deer, and hogs. She lives at the Edge of Hell. For real—that's the name of the haunted house where she spends her time.

Reticulated pythons are native to Southeast Asia. In captivity, as this one is (hopefully very securely), they can live up to 25 years. In 2018, the BBC reported that a snake two feet shorter than Medusa ate a woman in Indonesia while she was tending her vegetable garden. These snakes squeeze the life out of their victims then swallow them whole.

Guinness certified Medusa's hugeness in 2011, but because no one has challenged her grandeur, her handlers haven't measured her again—though her owners are sure she's bigger now. Currently, you may only visit the big girl during haunting season by visiting the Edge of Hell, but by 2021, Full Moon plans to have her in a habitat where she'll be visible year-round.

MEDUSA

What: World's longest snake in captivity

Where: 1401 W. 13th St., Kansas City, MO 64101

Cost: Free parking and hayrides, but haunted house tickets start at $27, with combo passes and line-skipping passes available for more.

Pro Tip: Check FullMoonProd.com for updates on Medusa.

Medusa the snake lives at The Edge of Hell and holds the record for the world's longest snake in captivity. Photos courtesy of Full Moon Productions

Guinness is making a new video of Medusa for promotional and social media purposes. Vice President Amber Arnett-Bequeaith says Medusa's recent pregnancy has delayed production.

STAY OFF THE SHOULDER

Why would someone build steps down to a highway?

Kansas City is not known for its stairways. No Spanish Steps. No *Rocky* steps leading up to the Philadelphia Museum of Art. No nail-less Loretto Chapel staircase like in Santa Fe. But here and there is a staircase of great mystery. Driving by on I-35 at 55 miles per hour, all that's visible is a bit of graffitied limestone retaining wall and a sliver of concrete staircase nestled in among the weeds and trees. It's only if you take exit 2W and drive around to the top at Summit Street and Kirk Drive that you can see the remains of what was once a thing of beauty.

This was West Terrace Park, a super fancy park in one of the city's first affluent neighborhoods, Quality Hill, overlooking the West Bottoms and built into a limestone bluff. Kersey Coates Drive used to run along the bottom of the lovely staircase, which gave pedestrians access to the park from the top or bottom of the bluff. The Park Board proposed its construction in 1893, but it wasn't until two years later that the Board assigned the design work to landscape mastermind George Kessler, according to writer Michael Wells. Even back then, though, a park board member was vocal in his certainty that the project was a waste of money. Rain, he insisted, would make the soil slide and cover the stairs, and retaining walls sturdy enough to hold the hill together would be expensive. That board member also didn't see the spot as a desirable hangout; Kessler would

A community group has been working since 2015 to re-beautify the spot, beginning by excavating the lower parts of the staircase that were covered in mud washed down the hill.

A staircase leads from I-35 to this park.

Palisades, Kersey Coates Drive, Kansas City, Mo.

This postcard shows the beauty of the original design. Photo courtesy of Missouri Valley Special Collections, Kansas City Public Library, Kansas City, Missouri

make it stunning to behold, but without a grandstand or the Victorian equivalent of Frisbee golf. No one listened to the park board member, though. By 1914, passenger trains had stopped running near enough for tourists to enjoy the site. In 1966, I-35 replaced the two-lane street, which totally ruined the vibe, because no one should ever walk down a staircase from a bluff and across an interstate highway.

A STAIRCASE

What: A mystery staircase that once connected a charming road to a charming park

Where: West Terrace Park, 750 Pennsylvania Ave., Kansas City, MO 64105

Cost: Free

Pro Tip: The staircase is visible from I-35 between exits 2W and 2X.

THE ABDUCTION OF KANSAS CITY'S FASHION MONARCH

All this happened to one woman?

Fashion designers aren't kidnapped for ransom very often. In the United States, it may have only happened once—here in Kansas City. From 1917 through 1957 Nell Donnelly—her label was Nelly Don—was the queen of Kansas City's textile industry, which, for a time, was second only to the textile industry of New York City. Reed was also one of the first self-made female millionaires in the nation, making her an excellent target in the eyes of local gangsters. In December of 1931, gangsters abducted her from the driveway of her home on Oak Street (which now houses the Kansas City Toy and Miniature Museum). The mobsters demanded $75,000 from her husband, Paul Donnelly, for her release. He contacted Senator James Reed, the family's lawyer, neighbor, and, perhaps unbeknownst to Paul, the father of Nell's child born earlier that year—after saying she was traveling to Europe that summer "to adopt." The senator mobilized the Kansas City police force and his friend Tom Pendergast's people, and rescuers found and freed Nell about 35 hours later. Not long after, she divorced Donnelly and married Reed, who, for propriety's sake, adopted his own biological son.

Kansas City's Garment District, at one time bustling with 5,000 or more workers, is now home to lofts and offices.

This giant button and needle stands as a memorial to the once-thriving Garment District.

Five house dresses by Nelly Don, 1922. Photo courtesy Wikimedia Commons

More than for her kidnapping, we remember Nell Donnelly Reed for revolutionizing her industry by introducing the idea of sewing clothes one section at a time, assembly-line style, rather than in the traditional way where one person saw a garment through from bolt to hanger. Little remains of the city's garment district, though a giant sewing needle acts as a memorial.

NELLY DON

What: A 22-foot high sewing needle poised to secure a big, red button created by Dave Stevens and installed in 2002

Where: 404 Eighth St., Kansas City, MO 64105

Cost: Free

Pro Tip: The dresses Nelly Don designed were the sort of thing June Cleaver wore on *Leave it to Beaver.*

LET'S MAKE THAT TACKY HILL DISAPPEAR

What's it take to set up a waterfall in a hotel lobby?

Driving along just about any Kansas City area highway, you'll spot tall bluffs of limestone that are the result of blasting away hills to make way for roads. But did you know that in the late 1960s, most of a hill was demolished to make room for part of a shopping and entertainment center? You can still see a bit of that hill in the lobby of the Westin Kansas City at Crown Center. That magnificent indoor waterfall in the lobby cascades down what's left of "Signboard Hill."

Signboard Hill was a spot not far from Liberty Memorial and across from Union Station that advertisers used to display . . . signs! All types of ads crowded the hill that was highly visible from a few major roads as well as to approaching passenger trains—and a lot of people thought it was terribly tacky. To make what we now know as Crown Center, the developers needed 85 acres, and the hill stood in the way. An article from the *Pitch* reports that Hallmark founder Joyce Hall especially hated Signboard Hill. Former Kansas Citian Walt Disney consulted on the project, but the master planner was Edward Larrabee Barnes, known for making buildings appear to grow out of the ground, and the hotel portion of the complex certainly looks that way.

Planners floated several names for the center before they landed on what we know today: Hall of Fame Place, Hall Town, Hallmark Hill, K. C. Circle, Crown Circle, Crowndale, and Gateway were some of the contenders.

Intersection of Main and Grand in 1927

Intersection of Pershing and Main in 1955. Photos courtesy of Missouri Valley Special Collections, Kansas City Public Library, Kansas City, Missouri

SIGNBOARD HILL

What: A hotel lobby that incorporated an existing hill and used it for a waterfall

Where: 1 E. Pershing Rd., Kansas City, MO 64108

Cost: Free

Pro Tip: Ride the hotel's glass elevators to look out over the city.

A NORMAN ROCKWELL OF OUR OWN!

Just how bad was that flood?

The man rolling up his sleeves over his giant arms seems to stretch high into the sky. An airplane flies near his head, and a tiny cow loiters around the man's calves, staring at the viewer. The man, who's holding blueprints, represents Kansas City itself, always ready to rally and rebuild after a disaster. This painting, *The Kansas City Spirit*, by iconic artist Norman Rockwell encouraged Kansas Citians after the great flood of 1951. Rockwell asked *Saturday Evening Post* artist John Atherton for help depicting the Kansas City skyline. This is the only painting he intentionally collaborated on.

When torrential rains caused massive flooding that July, Hallmark was still headquartered in the West Bottoms. According to Hallmark's website, J. C. Hall said: "By the time I got to the scene, our supplies were rolling down the river like confetti." Rockwell knew Hall and called to tell him how sorry he was for his loss. Rockwell later visited the city several times to conceptualize the painting. It's hard to say which of Kansas City's floods was the worst: the one in 1844, 1951, or 1993. Most would say 1951. The flood in 1844 may have been more colossal, but fewer homes and businesses dotted the city, so less damage could be done. After the 1951 flood, the city built new levees that curtailed the impact of 1993's nonstop rains for

Kansas City Spirit is the only painting Rockwell ever created alongside another artist, though he did hand off a piece called *Pittsfield Main St.* after his wife died.

Jessee Randall interviews Norman Rockwell as J. C. Hall stands by. Photo courtesy of Wilborn & Associates

Norman Rockwell at post-flood construction site. Photo courtesy of the Hallmark Archives, Hallmark Cards, Inc., Kansas City, Missouri

much of the town. According to Kansapedia, from July 9 to July 13, 1951, some areas in the Kansas River basin received 18.5 inches of rain.

NORMAN ROCKWELL PAINTING

What: Kansas City's very own Norman Rockwell painting

Where: Hallmark Visitors Center, 2501 McGee St., Kansas City, MO 64108

Cost: Free

Pro Tip: If you have children, make an appointment to visit Kaleidoscope while you're at Crown Center.

SOMETIMES TREES ARE PINK

But are those real leaves?

Who says a tree can't be pink? Yes, a real tree made of wood. A tree that grew up out of the ground from a seed, even. Swope Park has one. This one—and maybe there are others—is coated in glitter, and it has a name: *Tree, Broken Tree*. If you missed 2018's 10-week city-wide art exhibition Open Spaces, the tree will seem inordinately mysterious and wonderful to you. If you know about Open Spaces, it will remain wonderful, just not as mysterious.

The artist, Dylan Mortimer, is a former Kansas City area pastor. He has cystic fibrosis, and, in recent years, much of his art has dealt with bronchial tubes and lungs, so his installation at Swope Park is a "bronchial tree." When he turned 40, that felt like a miracle because his childhood doctors didn't think he'd make it through his teens; the average life expectancy of anyone with the disease is just 37 years. By 40, he'd already had two lung transplants. That's a total of three sets of lungs. He said that making art about lungs and bronchial tubes "was a way to transform a really ugly disease into something beautiful; that's what all the glitter is about—a really shiny material trying to transform a disease I was born with, with phlegm and blood." Mortimer said that all the visual art he's created about lungs

Though Mortimer selected a dead tree to paint, the power of glitter must have magically resuscitated it. Check it out in spring or summer to see its leaves.

Dylan Mortimer did not imagine the tree he painted pink would someday sprout leaves. Photo courtesy of Dylan Mortimer

and airways has allowed him to visualize healing from his disease in a new way. But how did the tree know to pitch in by growing new leaves?

TREE, BROKEN TREE

What: A pink tree

Where: South of the Southeast Community Center at 3999 Swope Pkwy. and E. Meyer Blvd., Kansas City, MO 64132

Cost: Free

Pro Tip: If you'd like to listen to the artist talk about his work, visit the archives of KCUR.org.

MURDER "MYSTERY" AND AN AMAZING MEMORIAL

You used to be able to buy cyanide and typhoid samples?

When I say "Swope," you say "Park." Try it: "Swope!" At least that's how it's done in Kansas City nowadays. However, 110 years ago, if I said "Swope," you might just shudder and ask, "Any news?" Thomas Swope was a real estate and mining millionaire who moved to Kansas City when he was 30 and started buying land, according to Jason Roe at the Kansas City Public Library. Swope was on the quiet side and never married, but he did live with his extended family in a mansion in Independence that's since been demolished. The family had a doctor named Bennett Clark Hyde who married Swope's niece, an heiress to the childless Swope's fortune. So when residents of the Swope house began dying, people had to wonder what was up. First, Swope's cousin (also the executor of his will) died. Two days later, Swope himself died of a "cerebral hemorrhage." But investigators later figured out that Hyde had administered Swope cyanide capsules for a few days in a row. Then Swope's nephew died of typhoid fever. Hyde had recently purchased typhoid samples, and somehow his family lived while nine members of the Swope clan did not. A jury convicted Hyde of the murders, and then later overturned the conviction. Probably the one thing he hadn't expected to happen, given the time

According to its website, Swope Park is made up of 1,805 acres and is one of the largest parks in the United States.

The Thomas Swope Memorial is guarded by two enormous lions.

SWOPE MURDERS

What: Thomas Swope Memorial

Where: 6900 Swope Memorial Dr., Kansas City, MO 64132

Cost: Free

Pro Tip: Swope's memorial affords a view of the park that you've probably never seen.

period, was Swope's niece to divorce him in 1920.

Swope Park is now home to Starlight Theater, the Kansas City Zoo, a nature center, a golf course, hundreds of acres of green space for playing, nine shelter houses for events, and a massive bandstand. Swope donated the park to Kansas City in 1896 and was interred at the Memorial in 1918, several years after his death. According to the Kansas City Public Library, 18,000 Kansas Citians showed up for the park's opening day.

RUINS FROM A FUTURE CIVILIZATION

What do you imagine will be built on this?

If you're cruising through Swope Park, say, off Golf Drive near the Swope Memorial, and you see the ruins of a future civilization, you are likely to be perplexed. That is understandable. The low, gleaming white stone walls meet at a right angle and are broken toward the long end. What's protocol? Sit on it? Steer clear in case it's haunted by future ghosts? It's hard to know.

What you're looking at is an art installation called *An Architectural Folly from a Future Place*. The R. C. Kemper Charitable Trust gifted it to the city. This is one of the few remaining installations from the 2018 Open Space*s* art exhibition, and it's okay to sit on it—nothing will reach around the corner and grab your leg. In her artist statement, Kansas City Art Institute assistant professor and chair of sculpture Jill Downen wrote that it's "a seemingly functional structure that in reality has no purpose other than to be the subject of contemplation."

According to Downen's website, she also has public installations in Mt. Vernon, Illinois, and St. Louis, Missouri. In her artist statement, she writes that her "art engages culture with silence, stillness, and a context to alter perception and return to the speed of life with measured focus." She goes on

Kansas City artist Jill Downen dreamed up this piece for Open Spaces, the city-wide art exhibition that took place during the summer of 2018.

Artist Jill Downen created what appears to be the ruins of a building's foundation.

ARCHITECTURAL FOLLY FROM A FUTURE PLACE

What: Ruins of a future civilization

Where: Swope Park just past the golf clubhouse

Cost: Free

Pro Tip: This is another out-of-the-way area. Don't visit alone.

to say that her art looks to the relationships between the body and architecture in terms of "construction, deterioration and restoration." Now throw that all into the future tense and you have something to think about while you sit on the future building's crumbling foundation.

THE PARK THAT JUST WON'T QUIT

You're sure those aren't ancient ruins?

Cave Spring Park ought to be rechristened "the little park that could." The 39 acres already have one alternate (and less fun) name: William M. Klein Park. The things that have happened to this recreational area would make any other park give up and become a strip mall. Volunteer caretaker Al Maddox told the *Star* that vandals tore apart the cabins and burned their remains to the ground in the 1940s, which explains the eerie chimneys—still standing. The place looks like the ruins of an ancient civilization. He also said that park planners dammed seven acres of the park to create a lake from the natural springs, but again, vandals struck and dynamited the dam. The whole lake drained into the surrounding countryside.

Now, the park is well loved by the neighborhood and the Boy Scouts, and coming upon its idyllic bubbling brook is a peaceful experience. The aboveground cave mouth is the best part, though. You're likely to notice a well-made sign about Corky and

CAVE SPRING PARK

What: Park with a natural spring, waterfall, and aboveground cave entrance

Where: 8701 E. Gregory Blvd., Raytown, MO 64133

Cost: Free

Pro Tip: Wear good walking shoes that can get dirty—the park's trails are rustic.

According to the *Kansas City Star*, Harry Truman's grandfather owned some of the property in the late 1800s before its incarnation as a golf course and resort in the 1920s.

These chimneys used to heat resort cabins in Cave Spring Park. Now they're only a little creepy.

Tim. You'll definitely wonder about it. Harold C. (Corky) Maddox (the caretaker's brother) died in 2012. His son, Tim, passed away first. The sign is a tribute to them.

MAUSOLEUMS: THEY'RE NOT JUST FOR THE DEAD

Is it nice in here, or what?

Think hard. Have you ever walked around in a mausoleum? A dark, damp, somewhat chilly crypt where real people are entombed in the walls? Kansas City has quite a few proper mausoleums, most from the late 1800s and early 1900s when it was hot to memorialize oneself that way, before the cost became too prohibitive even for the wealthy. Elmwood Cemetery has 29 mausoleums, for instance. Forest Hill has a pretty darn big one. William Rockhill Nelson and his family are in one at Mt. Washington Cemetery that looks like a church. You can find a super-haunted one at Forest Hill. If you visit that one, take a tall person with you who can reach a phone over the plywood blocking the entrance to make a video that shows the empty tombs up and down the walls. However, most of these places are locked up tight.

MT. MORIAH MAUSOLEUM

What: Mausoleums

Where: Mt. Moriah, 10507 Holmes Rd., Kansas City, MO 64131

Cost: Free

Pro Tip: Goodness knows I'm not your mom, but use your best manners if you visit.

Several famous people are buried in the cemetery surrounding Mt. Moriah Mausoleum, including Walter Cronkite, Dan Quisenberry, and Russell Stover.

The Mt. Moriah Mausoleum is an art deco masterpiece.

So, if mausoleum visiting is on your to-do list, check out one you can actually walk around in. Mt. Moriah is well maintained, only sort of creepy, really beautiful inside, and filled with lovely art deco stained glass. It was completed in 1926 in the style of Egypt's ancient Temple of Karnak, and two large sphinxes guard the entrance.

A NEGLECTED PIECE OF THE WHITE HOUSE

But isn't that just a chunk of concrete?

During President Harry S. Truman's renovation of the White House, he authorized a souvenir program that aimed to distribute the historic construction debris to interested parties. Items of real historical significance went to museums, but other detritus such as boards and bits of unmarked stone went to people and institutions who were just interested in having a piece of history. One of those pieces is here in Kansas City at the now-closed Southwest High School. The damaged, unmarked piece at the high school is at the north end of the football field near the alley. Its information plaque is nearby on the base of the flagpole, a move made decades ago so that more people would see the plaque, according to *The Rise and Fall of Excellence* by alumnus Edward Matheny.

WHITE HOUSE FOUNDATION STONE

What: A piece of the original White House

Where: Southwest High School, 6512 Wornall Rd., Kansas City, MO 64113

Cost: Free

Pro Tip: The foundation stone is at the northeast end and the flagpole is at the northwest end of the field.

The still-active alumni association is trying to figure out what to do about the chunk of 1600 Pennsylvania Avenue and the plaque now that the high school is closed.

In grateful memory of
Louis A. House, who
coached football, basketball
and track at Southwest High
School, 1925-1955. His teams
were perennial city champions.
Thanks to President Truman,
the stones in this monument
were from the original White
House prior to 1812 and were
recovered in the course of
extensive reconstruction during
President Truman's Administration.

Inscription by the class of 1935

The Southwest High School Class of
1935 dedicated this chunk of the White
House to Coach Louis A. House.

According to Matheny, a man named Henry Talge had been friends with Truman, so Truman sent Talge a pre-1812 piece of White House foundation stone. Talge's grandson was close to the high school's longtime coach, Louis House, and when House died in 1955, the Talge family decided to donate the stone to the school as a memorial to him.

SAY, WHO INVITED THE EGYPTOLOGIST?

Does this qualify as Egyptian?

Ever since Napoleon's Egyptian campaign back in the late 1790s, Western culture has enjoyed adding Egyptian flourishes to architecture and art. Use of the style waxed and waned through the 1800s, but the discovery of King Tutankhamun's tomb in 1922 threw decorators and architects into "Egyptomania," according to the Metropolitan Museum of Art's website. It's therefore peculiar that Atchison, Kansas, which is still pretty far out in the country but was really far out in the country 100 years ago, has a large Egyptian room in its Masonic Temple. The Masons built the temple in 1915, *before* Egyptomania.

Johnson County–based Egyptologist Stacy Davidson says that the Masonic Lodge in Atchison may have consulted with Shriners in the construction of their temple because Shriners use Egyptian symbols in their ceremonies. But that's just a guess. What Davidson does know for sure is that the Egyptian-themed room is as big as a tomb or a small chapel, and just about everything in it is wrong. For starters, the colors and style are off. She says: "Imagine seeing an American flag, but instead of red, white, and blue, there is purple, green, and orange, and there aren't 13 stripes but 11, and they aren't stripes but wavy lines, and instead of stars there are daisies." She says the sphinxes in the room are not properly Egyptian, resembling

---

MASONIC TEMPLE

What: An ode to an Egyptian temple within Atchison's Masonic Lodge

Where: 121 1/2 N. Fifth St., Atchison, KS 66002

Cost: Free

Pro Tip: Call Jayson Huff at 573-366-1163 to schedule a visit.

The details of this sphinx and engraving in Atchison's Masonic Temple are unusual according to an Egyptologist. Photos courtesy of Stacy Davidson

no pharaoh she's familiar with. Then there's the typo-laden Hebrew script on the stained glass. Davidson says including the 10 Commandments in that setting probably has something to do with the Exodus story, but again, she's got to throw up her hands and say she's not sure.

"The figures are cartoonish. The Egyptians had a particular grid system that they used for proportions and scene composition."
—Egyptologist Stacy Davidson

THE WELL-TRAVELED TREE

How could this tree have been to the moon?

Hundreds of visitors to outer space have been living around the globe, hiding in forests and parks, for decades. They go by many names: loblolly pine, redwood, sweet gum, sycamore, and Douglas fir. They are trees now, but when they were only tiny seeds, Command Pilot Stuart Roosa packed them in a little can and stowed them in his spacecraft. On January 31, 1971, Roosa and the seeds left the earth on Apollo 14. Eventually those little seeds orbited Earth 34 times. Apollo 14 was the third moon landing, but it was Alan Shepard and Edgar Mitchell who actually walked on the lunar surface; Roosa stayed in orbit. In all, Roosa brought about 500 seeds, 450 of which the US Forest Service later sprouted—no one was sure if, having left the earth, the trees would achieve typical growth for their varieties, but they did.

In 1976, the Forest Service distributed the saplings to parks, colleges, government offices, heads of state, and dignitaries as gifts across the world for America's bicentennial. But most were lost in the shuffle; 450 is a lot of trees. According to NASA, David Williams, a curator at the National Space Science Data Center in Greenbelt, Maryland, has taken on the task of locating as many of the "moon trees" as possible. As of April 2019, he'd located only 81. Fortunately for the Kansas City area, one well-documented moon tree, a sycamore, lives in Atchison,

In addition to the moon tree, the forest features trees from every state and 36 territories and countries around the world.

This grand old American Sycamore has orbited the moon.

Kansas, in the International Forest of Friendship, itself an unexpected feature of the landscape. A group called the Ninety-Nines (the international organization of women pilots), along with the Kansas State University Forestry Extension, the City of Atchison, and Joe Carrigan and Fay Gillis Wells, established the park in 1976.

MOON TREE

What: A tree that orbited the moon

Where: International Forest of Friendship, Allingham Dr., Atchison, KS 66002

Cost: Free

Pro Tip: Give yourself time to read all the names and tree-related quotations along the path.

LOUISBURG: CIDER AND APEX PREDATORS

You expected squirrels in Louisburg, but did you know about the tigers?

Louisburg, Kansas, is a field-trip favorite in the Kansas City metro. But most visitors hit either the cider mill or one of the several wineries in the surrounding area—and may or may not even know about the tigers in the woods. This town of 4,500 is home to about 28 predators, some of which are apex predators, including seven tigers, two lions, and two wolves. But this is no zoo, it's Cedar Cove Feline Conservation & Education Center. Most of the animals have heartbreaking histories: one tiger toured the nation as a performer, spending 10 hours a day in a van, chained by his neck to a pole in order to strengthen his back legs for performances; a couple purchased an African leopard at an exotic animal auction then declawed him so he could be a house cat; a mountain lion rode in the cab of a semi as a kitten, then did a stint as the mascot of a bar; several bobcats, foxes, and wolves got so used to eating scraps in people's backyards that they no longer feared humans, making them vulnerable and unable to live in the wild. About 20 volunteers run the facility; no one profits except for the creatures.

According to a tour guide at the Cedar Cove Feline Conservation & Education Center, founder William Pottorff grew up in Louisburg loving animals. It was during a tour in Vietnam that he fell in love with the Siberian Tiger and witnessed the ruin of its habitat.

Pottorff was an Army veteran who did two tours in Vietnam and received two Purple Hearts for his actions. He ran Cedar Cove until his death in 2012.

Olivia, a 5-year-old Bengal tiger rescue, lounges in the grass at Cedar Cove.

Voodoo, a 19-year-old leopard the sanctuary adopted at 5 1/2 months after a couple tried making a house pet out of him. Photos courtesy of Steve Klein

CEDAR COVE

What: Large cat (and some other creatures) sanctuary and rehab center

Where: 3783 K68 Hwy., Louisburg, KS 66053

Cost: Weather permitting, tickets are $9 for adults, $7 for seniors and children up to 12, and free for kids under 4.

Pro Tip: Hours of operation vary by season. Call ahead (913-837-5515) or visit the website (SaveOurSiberians.org) to ensure you don't make the trip for nothing. See the cider mill while you're in Louisburg.

151

MISSOURI'S WHERE IT'S AT

Where's the best place to be at the end of the world? (You already know the answer.)

Not to oversimplify, or in this case, under-complicate, this bit of Missouri history, but it's worth noting that until 1977, a state executive order allowed the extermination of Mormons. Executive Order 44 reads: "The Mormons must be treated as enemies, and must be exterminated or driven from the state, if necessary, for the public peace—their outrages are beyond all description." Wow. Missouri governor Lilburn Boggs issued the order in 1838 after thousands of Mormons moved to the area around Independence. Like Mike Bickle (of International House of Prayer fame), the church's founder Joseph Smith had received his own order from God a few years earlier telling him to move from New York to Missouri because the promised land was around Independence and the second coming of Christ would also take place there, according to Michael Scherer, coauthor of *The Journey of a People*. Many historic spots remain today, such as the Far West Temple site where there's a church and a memorial to those who took the journey.

Remember that this was when the religion was very new; Smith and the gang didn't have much to differentiate them from any other leader and group of followers. The existing settlers were not comfortable with what seemed like an invasion.

After the Missourians forced the Mormons out of Far West, the group built another temple in Nauvoo, Illinois, continuing to hope "that they would one day return to reclaim these sacred lands in Missouri prior to the Second Coming."

The Far West Historic Site includes a still operational chapel and a large memorial.

FAR WEST

What: One of northwestern Missouri's several Mormon sites

Where: NW State Hwy. D, Kingston, MO 64650

Cost: Free

Pro Tip: The chapel is across the highway from the historic site. Be careful crossing!

Additionally, Missourians had already spent some time converting Native Americans to Christianity. When thousands of Mormons arrived, they had the same intention and began trying to teach the Native people an even different doctrine. Long story short, the Missourians told the Mormons they could only stay in the area if they'd live and work within the boundaries of Caldwell County. Before long, the county wasn't big enough, and the Mormons started doing as they pleased. Eventually, both sides formed militias and spent time shooting each other.

ALL HAIL, PRESIDENT ATCHISON

Whom should we believe?

Be honest: If you were president for a day, what would you do? Free a bunch of your lunatic friends and family members from prison? Choose a new paint color for the White House? Throw a giant party and invite all of your favorite celebrities? Finally meet Cher? No? David Rice Atchison didn't do any of that either. In fact, he slept through about half of his presidency.

Let's go back in time to March 4, 1849—David's big day. He was already a senator, and the US Senate website says some other senators had previously tapped him to act as president pro tempore 13 times (meaning he presided over the senate while the vice president was busy). It was no surprise to anyone, then, when the senate elected him again on March 2, the Friday before President Zachary Taylor's inauguration. Presidential, senatorial, and congressional terms used to begin at noon on March 4 every year, but that date in 1849 was a Sunday, so the nation's capital was closed for business. President Taylor's inauguration was at noon on March 5. So who was president from noon on Sunday until noon on Monday? Many, including Atchison himself, said he was.

This statue of someone who may or may not have been a president of the United States stands outside the Clinton County Courthouse in Missouri.

DAVID RICE ATCHISON
1807 — 1886
PRESIDENT OF UNITED STATES
ONE DAY
LAWYER, STATESMAN AND JURIST
U. S. SENATE 1843 — 1855

ERECTED BY STATE OF MISSOURI
MEMORIAL COMMISSION
SENATOR B. T. GORDON, CHAIRMAN
REPRESENTATIVE HUGH M. MARSH
JOSEPH E. BLACK, MEMBER

Terms of public office all expired at noon on March 4, so technically, Atchison wasn't in office on that day any more than anyone else was.

KILL CREEK ISN'T THAT SCARY

Or is it?

It's a fact that the human mind wants a story. If we only have part of the picture, we'll fill in the blanks, consciously or subconsciously. Writer Scott Thomas took that a little further than the average person would, though. For years, while he was a student at the University of Kansas, the Coffeyville native passed the Kill Creek Road exit on Highway 10 between Johnson and Douglas Counties. He decided the road must lead to a terrifying, abandoned house. Then he did what most others would not: he wrote a novel called *Kill Creek*. The novel is about four famous horror writers who agree to spend Halloween night together in a haunted house. What could go wrong with a setup like that?

Thomas told KCUR 89.3's Central Standard talk show: "When you're in the country, or you drive by an old house, and clearly someone lived there at some point, things happened

KILL CREEK ROAD SIGN

What: A road called Kill Creek

Where: The sign is visible from KS 10 between Douglas and Johnson Counties.

Cost: Free except for gas

Pro Tip: Thomas has another really frightening book called *Violet*.

The word "kill" isn't what you think. It's from a Middle Dutch word that means riverbed or channel. So Thomas's scary sign translates to something much duller along the lines of "Creek Creek."

Author Scott Thomas wondered about this sign for years before writing a book about it. Photo courtesy of Scott Thomas

there, but now the windows are all broken out, and the roof is caving in, and you start to wonder what happened there. The house is full of memories for someone; they could be good, they could be bad, but now it's kind of been forgotten, but it's still there, it still exists."

FICTIONAL TENNESSEE TOWN WITH ITS ROOTS IN KANSAS

Just what happened in Limetown?

The tiny fictional village of Limetown, Tennessee, became a ghost town in a matter of moments. Over 300 men, women, and children disappeared without a trace, and millions of Limetown podcast subscribers have bitten their fingernails clear to the quick alongside narrator Lia Haddock, trying to make sense of the cryptic clues left behind by the bizarre community of science's top minds. Was Limetown a cult? Was it an attempt at a utopian society? A hippie commune? Did aliens lift the people into the heavens, or did they merely relocate, leaving behind all of their earthly possessions?

One man in particular, Cote Smith, has worked extra hard to make sense of the eerie tale. Smith is a novelist from Leavenworth who now lives in Lawrence. Zack Akers and Skip Bronkie, who'd invented the original storyline for a podcast, selected Smith to go back in time 10 years before the events of Limetown and explain circumstances leading up to the mass disappearance. Smith did that work admirably, and while he was at it, he inserted a whole lot of Kansas into the story. For instance, Menninger, the psychiatric clinic that operated in Topeka for 77 years before its move to Houston in 2003, became the name of a lab connected to Limetown, though

---

The Limetown podcast began in 2013 and ran as a TV show on Facebook Watch for a couple months in 2019.

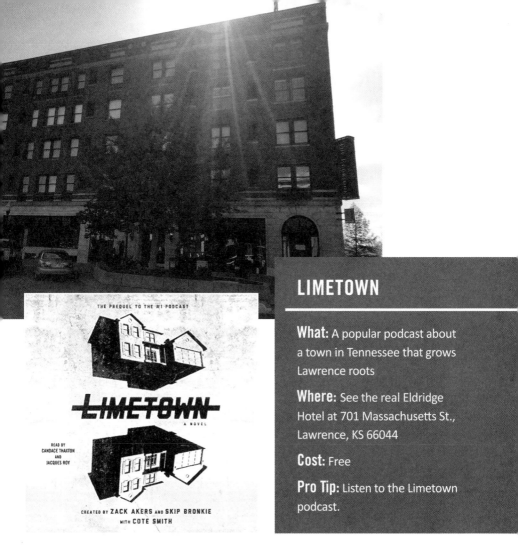

LIMETOWN

What: A popular podcast about a town in Tennessee that grows Lawrence roots

Where: See the real Eldridge Hotel at 701 Massachusetts St., Lawrence, KS 66044

Cost: Free

Pro Tip: Listen to the Limetown podcast.

The Eldridge Hotel in Lawrence wound up in a book Cote Smith wrote about the fictional Limetown. Book jacket photo courtesy of Amazon

Smith relocated it to Australia. Lawrence's historic Eldridge Hotel pops up in Colorado as the creepy home to a bunch of geniuses performing psychological experiments on anyone they can capture. The characters themselves are even from Lawrence.

159

JOHNSON COUNTY'S ARMY BASE

You say land ripe for retail is just sitting empty?

It's very easy to find information about the Sunflower Ammunition Plant in northwestern Johnson County, Kansas, but it's tough to properly imagine it. Both the *Kansas City Star* and the Johnson County Museum try to help our collective imagination by comparing the 15-square-mile property to another of the same size within county limits: Leawood, one of the wealthiest cities in the state's wealthiest county. Except where Leawood is jam-packed with mini-mansions, coffee shops, and dog spas, the Sunflower Ammunition Plant is home only to prairie grass, broken-down shacks, cracked roads, and contaminated waste. Sunflower Redevelopment Group bought the property in 2005.

But the US Army was the original landlord, which is also very unusual for Johnson County. In 1942, the base was one of the world's biggest producers of "smokeless gunpowder and propellants for small arms, cannons and rockets," according to the *Star*. It employed as many as 24,000 people at its peak of operations. To keep up the Leawood comparison, 16,000 people worked there in 2017, according to Data USA. The Johnson County Museum describes the barbed wire–encased property: "Its infrastructure included a power plant, a water treatment plant, a hospital, a fire department, a security force, over 100

A 2019 *Star* report suggests that the land will be ready for building between 2021 and 2028, after more than $200 million of decontamination work is complete.

One of the entrances to the Sunflower Ammunition Plant In Johnson County, Kansas

"Follow the Road to Safety." *Don't do it!*

SUNFLOWER AMMUNITION PLANT

What: A massive ghost Army base in Johnson County

Where: 35425 W. 103rd St, De Soto, KS 66018

Cost: Free

Pro Tip: Don't try to enter the base.

miles of paved roads, and 70 miles of railroad track." What's going on there now? Since it closed in 1992, the Army has been trying to clean up the hazardous materials on the valuable property with easy highway access. Developers weep openly about the unused acreage and will continue to do so until it's clean. For many years, the county hoped for an Oz-themed amusement park in that spot.

BRICKLAYING: A SPECTATOR SPORT?

Don't you just love brick roads?

Here and there around downtown Olathe, Kansas, walkers and drivers can enjoy lovely brickwork. Most of the buildings are made of brick, brick strips along the roads accent the sidewalks, and a massive brick design graces the intersection of Cherry and Santa Fe Streets. It was, after all, bricks that paved the way for the modern road. But don't we long for the time when whole roads were made of brick? None of this asphalt and concrete business like we have now—no, sir! A solid brick road like on Disney World's Main Street is certainly more charming than black asphalt and calls to mind soda shops and horse-drawn carriages. But you know who gets lost when nostalgia rears its head? The bricklayer. According to an article in *The Best Times*, a Johnson County government magazine, a single man was responsible for a great deal of Johnson County's original brick paving. The man was known as "Indian Jim," a member of the Oneida Nation who did some of his best work in the 1920s.

The Best Times cites an account of a bricklaying contest in a newspaper of the period called the *Johnson County Democrat*. Jim won the contest by paving 416 feet of Kansas City road in 7 hours and 48 minutes with 46,664 eight-pound bricks. He laid 100 bricks a minute and won $200 plus his hourly wage of $2 per hour. If students at Olathe North High School hadn't decided

Jim's real name was James Garfield Cleveland Brown, and local newspapers bragged that he was the very best bricklayer in the Midwest.

A modest memorial to a hardworking man

Top: James Garfield Cleveland Brown, 1869–1955. Photo courtesy of Lenexa Historical Society

Bottom: Brown also paved the streets in Texas. Photo courtesy of Lenexa Historical Society

BRICKWORK

What: Monument to Jim the bricklayer and lovely brickwork in downtown Olathe

Where: The marker is at Poplar Street and Kansas City Road; enter downtown at Cherry and Santa Fe Streets.

Cost: Free

Pro Tip: Downtown Olathe is another charming place to walk around and find a bite to eat.

to honor Jim with a marker located at Poplar Street and Kansas City Road in 2007, the man may have otherwise been lost in Johnson Countians' daydreams of more "charming" times.

FORGET OUTER SPACE, HE FLEW *HERE* FIRST.

Where did John Glenn get those mad skills?

Governments the world over have honored astronaut John Glenn (1921–2016) with street and bridge names, parks, schools, a US Navy ship, a fireboat, an airport, a NASA research center, and many other things. According to *USA Today*, Glenn orbited the earth more than 130 times, but his first three times in 1962 were the first for any American. Two Russians were the first humans to orbit.

Recently Olathe, Kansas, named a street for him—John Glenn Way—and dedicated it on July 16, 2019. Why now? And why Olathe? Well, for starters, a road at the local airport, New Century AirCenter, simply didn't have a name. But more importantly, the county decided to honor him at the AirCenter because that's where Glenn learned to fly in 1942 back when it was the Olathe Naval Air Station. He was part of the Olathe Naval Air Station's first graduating class. Much later, when Glenn was 77 years old, he became the oldest person to ever attempt space travel. In 1998 he spent 90 days in space as part of NASA program on aging.

According to the *Gardner News*, TV game show host Bob Barker also trained as a pilot at the Air Station. The base closed in 1970 after more than 27 years of training pilots.

JOHN GLENN WAY

What: A street in Olathe named for John Glenn

Where: John Glenn Way is near the intersection of Prairie Village Drive and Moonlight Road in Olathe.

Cost: Free

Pro Tip: This will impress your friends: According to WingsOverKansas.com, Glenn's nickname was "Magnet Ass."

This street sign acts as a small tribute to an American pioneer.

John Glenn. Photo courtesy of Wikimedia Commons

John Glenn earned his wings on a two-seater Stearman Plane in Johnson County.

THINK TWICE BEFORE SHOWING OFF

Where'd my sign go?

You've heard of old ladies' purses being stolen, but their special-order aluminum signs? That's just what happened to Merriam's Myra Jenks in 2015. But it wasn't exactly any old special-order aluminum sign—no, it was one she'd wanted for decades, one that she'd written and published a book to raise money for. Her special sign commemorated a plane crash that terrified residents of Merriam, Kansas, during World War II.

During the war, it's pretty safe to say that a good number of the bombers that crashed did so over enemy territory. However, Jenks told the *Shawnee Mission Post* that in July 1944, when she was 21 years old, someone ran into her workplace to tell her that a B-24 (Liberator bomber) had crashed near her house, destroying five homes. As Jenks tells it, the pilot, Kenny Keech, was performing his last test run before shipping off. His instructor at an airfield in Nebraska told him he could fly anywhere he wanted. He chose his hometown. He and his crew circled Merriam lower and lower, waving at the frightened and concerned citizenry below. Witnesses reported seeing the crew's laughing faces through the windows; however, Keech had flown too low for correction. Onboard, three men died and three others suffered critical injuries, along with three people on the ground.

Pilot Keech's family said no to the idea of a plaque; the memory was too terrible, and they didn't want a permanent public reminder. Jenks let it rest for 20 years before raising the funds.

WWII PLANE CRASHES INTO HOMES

The crash site of the B-24J Liberator Bomber on July 26, 1944, damaging four homes and destroying a fifth; topping several trees, downing electric and telephone lines and scattering plane parts over several blocks. This resulted in injuries to three civilians, major injuries to three crewmen, and the death of the other three crewmen.

In memory of the crewmen killed:

Lt. James B. Davis - Oklahoma City, OK
Cpl. Calvin H. Somers - Brownsville, PA
Cpl. E.G. Vellone - Syracuse, NY

Historic Merriam 2014

This sign memorializes the crash of a World War II bomber in 1944 that killed three out-of-staters.

WORLD WAR II PLANE CRASH MEMORIAL

What: A sign in Merriam commemorating the crash of an overzealous World War II pilot

Where: It's next to a bench on Antioch Road near the entrance to Cinemark Theater.

Cost: Free

Pro Tip: The bench is positioned beneath shade trees. Sit a spell.

So, Jenks wanted a commemorative plaque. In her 90s, she raised $1,000 to finally buy the sign. The city installed it in 2014, but less than a year later, someone ran off with it. Ultimately, the city replaced the sign.

GRAVES TO CONSIDER WHILE YOU DINE

Would you like a sprinkle of mortality on your deli meat?

After the Mr. Goodcents employee in Mission, Kansas, splashes oil and vinegar on your lunchmeat and adds a dash of salt and pepper, sit at the table closest to the intersection and puzzle over the tiny cemetery just outside the window. It's called Cross Cemetery; Washington and Nancy Cross are buried there. Washington died in 1872 at the exact age of 62 years, 11 months, and five days. Nancy died in 1886 at 76 years, 11 months, and 19 days. Online sources disagree about the spelling of the last name: some argue that the first letter is a "G." Gross indeed.

Their little plot is nice enough, sandwiched, if you will, between the two busy streets on a patch of grass and backed by a wrought iron fence. A marker dedicates the plots to "the pioneers of this community," and they were the pioneers. Kansas joined the Union in 1861. These two were most likely newly settled in the area where the road to California branched off from the Santa Fe Trail and headed west. Their fellow pioneers might be buried in the Mr. Goodcents parking lot and under the street. Only the Crosses' headstones remain.

At the end of the 1800s, it was common practice for rural families to use a corner of their pastureland as a family cemetery.

These graves crowd up against Mr. Goodcents in Mission, Kansas.

According to Craig Crease of the Kansas City Area Historic Trails Association, the 1902 Johnson County Atlas shows that the Cross family owned a great deal of land around what became the intersection.

CROSS FAMILY CEMETERY

What: A tiny cemetery awfully close to the seating area of a sandwich place

Where: 6250 Johnson Dr., Mission, KS 66202

Cost: Just the cost of your lunch if you go inside.

Pro Tip: Play it cool so you don't worry the other customers.

AN INVISIBLE BOAT ANCHORED IN A DRIED-UP SEA

What's next, a fossil of an anchor?

Tool around Mission, Kansas, long enough, and you'll encounter a three-ton Danforth anchor. Any good Midwesterner who's ever looked at the ground while she walks can tell you the region is full of sea-life fossils. You've got your standard-issue impressions of guys such as *Delocrinus*, *Acanthoceras*, and *Meganeuropsis*, but also creatures more people have heard of such as clams, coral, and here and there a shark. But even though the Western Interior Seaway covered the Midwest—Kansas was toward the middle, as it tends to be—no one really expects to run across an actual anchor.

Prior to 2004, the anchor was in the possession of the US Navy in Williamsburg, Virginia. It appeared one day in this sleepy, well-kept suburban neighborhood as if it had dropped from the sky, unlike the marine fossils everyone is so accustomed to. Well, it didn't really fall from the sky. The Navy was nice enough to donate it for the August 15, 2004, dedication ceremony of Mission's Pearl Harbor Survivors Memorial Park on the 63rd anniversary of V-J Day, commemorating victory over Japan in World War II. The memorial was created at the behest of the local chapter of the Pearl Harbor Survivors Association, and it also includes a bench

---

The Pearl Harbor Survivors Association was founded in 1958 and disbanded in 2011. The last Kansas City–area member, Dorwin Lamkin, died in March 2019 at the age of 96.

PEARL HARBOR
DECEMBER 7, 1941
DEDICATED V-J DAY
AUGUST 15, 2004

PEARL HARBOR
MEMORIAL PARK

A large ship's anchor in a Kansas suburb seems out of place until you see that it's a Pearl Harbor memorial.

PEARL HARBOR MEMORIAL PARK

What: An anchor in a neighborhood

Where: The corner of Martway and Maple Street in Mission, Kansas

Cost: Free

Pro Tip: The anchor is near Kansas City's best spot for buffalo wings, The Peanut.

with chapter members' names, all of whom are now deceased, and an encased piece of the USS *Arizona*'s aft deckhouse superstructure.

KANSAS'S LONE KENTUCKY DERBY WINNER

There's a horse buried where?

Though Lawrin only lived to the age of 20, he had dozens and dozens of children with 90 different baby mamas. If he'd been human, this would have been alarming, but Lawrin had won the 1938 Kentucky Derby, and with that glory came certain expectations. Forty-seven of his colts grew up to win races, and two were stakes holders. The best among them was named Historian. As of this printing, Lawrin remains the only Kentucky Derby winner bred in Kansas.

In 1921, Herbert Woolf, president of Woolf Brothers Clothing, bought 320 acres in what would become Prairie Village, Kansas, according to the Corinth Hills Home Association. He named it Woolford Farm. In 1955, real estate developer J. C. Nichols bought Woolford Farm and began subdividing the land

KENTUCKY DERBY WINNER'S GRAVE

What: A Kentucky Derby winner buried in a cul-de-sac

Where: Corinth Downs at 59 Le Mans Court in Prairie Village

Cost: Free

Pro Tip: Please be considerate of Lawrin's neighbors when you pay your respects.

The American Classic Pedigrees website writes that Lawrin was a "robust bay colt of staying type . . . tall . . . workmanlike, and plain in appearance. . . . He was a gluttonous eater."

This graveyard is a jarring sight in this tiny cul-de-sac.

Lawrin with jockey Eddie Arcaro in 1938. This photo is encased at the gravesite. Photo courtesy of Jay Senter

into the Corinth Hills neighborhoods. It was only natural that Lawrin be buried on the farm. It's not so natural that today the poor horse is actually buried in a subdivision.

YOUR LOCAL AIRPLANE SALVAGE YARDS

Where can I get airplane parts around here?

Two of the nation's four major aircraft salvage yards are within an hour of Kansas City: Dodson in Rantoul, Kansas, and White Industries in Bates City, Missouri. The airplane parts business is just about as niche as it gets—management must know detailed histories of all the parts as well as the newest Federal Aviation Administration (FAA) rules. So now that Terry White, owner of White Industries since 1956, would like to sell and retire, he's—how shall we say—grounded.

White is in his early 80s and in possession of a working private airport (the Harry S. Truman Regional Airport), 178 acres, and about 2,000 aircraft. In 2014, *Corporate Jet Investor* announced that the property, with everything on it, was up for sale. But in early 2020, White still hadn't had anything but offers for the land itself, which he turned down; he wants someone to take over the business, not simply buy the property. Adding to White's challenges, since January 2020, the FAA has required an upgrade

White Industries aircraft salvage yard. Photo courtesy of White Industries

to all aircraft called ADS-B Out, allowing planes as well as ground vehicles to communicate their location, speed, and identification to each other and aircraft controllers. If the cost to upgrade older planes is too high, salvage yards may see an increase in outdated planes, which are difficult to sell. Then what's White going to do?

The other two major airplane salvage yards are not far away either. They're in Oklahoma and Alabama.

I LOVE THIS STORY SO MUCH, I'LL NAME A TOWN AFTER IT

What do you mean they didn't know she was their mother?

Who hasn't used the amusing catchphrase: "Dead, dead, and never called me mother"? Goodness only knows how many times I've said it! Just kidding—I'd never even heard it until I started looking into the town of East Lynne, Missouri, in Cass County—population approximately 303. East Lynne was founded in 1871, and, according to 1917's *The History of Cass County, Missouri* by Allen Glenn, the founding fathers (or mothers) named it after an "old play of the same name."

A novel entitled *East Lynne*, by Ellen Wood, came out in England just 10 years before the town in Missouri put down stakes. Some time in the intervening years, creative-types adapted the novel for the stage (at least nine times), and the staged versions became worldwide crowd-pleasers. The story was about a woman leaving her husband and children for her lover. But wait! After she bears the lover's child (a love child), the rapscallion leaves her! So she disguises herself and moves back in with her original family as a housekeeper. They don't notice, of course, a lot like no one suspected the titular

---

The British Library website says that for 40 years, almost constantly, some company in the English-speaking world was performing *East Lynne*—the catchphrase was one of the most famous parts.

East Lynne's railroad depot in 1957. Photo courtesy of Springfield-Greene County

EAST LYNNE, MO

What: A town named after a novel

Where: East Lynne, MO 64743

Cost: Free

Pro Tip: Lucky for us, the full text of this book is available for free on gutenberg.org.

Frontispiece from an 1883 printing of the novel East Lynne. *Photo courtesy of Wikimedia Commons*

character in *Mrs. Doubtfire* was simply the children's father in a wig and dress. The schtick never gets old. It does appear that East Lynne is the only town in the world named after the masterpiece.

OUR RADICAL, VEGETARIAN FOREFATHERS

Why *wouldn't* a vegetarian colony be established in Kansas?

Englishman Henry Clubb was a soft-hearted, odd sort of duck. He was one of the founding fathers of modern Western vegetarianism back in the mid-1800s. According to research by Aaron Barnhart and Diane Eickhoff, Clubb thought vegetarianism was so important that he convinced about 100 people to send him money to establish a special meat-free colony just south of present-day Humboldt, Kansas. Clubb and his followers attempted to set up their utopia in Osage territory in 1856, five years before Kansas became a state. He wanted the four-square-mile city laid out in an octagon with an octagonal building at its center that would serve as a common area.

Much of Barnhart and Eickhoff's information comes from the stupendously titled account of the short-lived experiment by a New Yorker named Miriam Colt, whose family followed Clubb to Kansas. Her book, available online, is called *Went to Kansas; Being a Thrilling Account of an Ill-Fated Expedition to That Fairy Land, and its Sad Results*. By the time Colt and family arrived at the site of the little village, she was pretty mad. She wrote: "Now we all have come! have brought our fathers, our mothers, and our little ones, and find no shelter sufficient to shield them from the furious prairie winds, and the terrific storms of the

---

Iola Register columnist Bob Johnson owns the colony's site now.

Nothing much remains of the great experiment. Photo courtesy of Trevor Hoag

climate!" Clubb had failed to prepare even basic shelter for his pilgrims; many of them died. The whole affair was over in a matter of months.

VEGETARIAN COLONY

What: A vegetarian colony

Where: A marker is just north of Highway 169 on the road to Humboldt, Kansas. The small marker is at the actual site and is east of the corner of 1300 Road and Alabama Road/250th along the Allen-Neosho line. The stone marker is north of the junction of old Highway 169 and new Highway 169, also known as the Humboldt/Chanute exit.

Cost: Free

Pro Tip: Somewhere in the area is, or was, a small body of water named Vegetarian Creek. Let me know if you find it!

OLDEST MOVIE THEATER IN THE WORLD

But is the popcorn fresh?

The oldest movie theater in the entire world is not in Paris, London, Budapest, or New York City. It's right here in Ottawa, Kansas, and it's called Plaza 1907. The *Guinness Book of World Records* certified it, so don't even try to say you've heard of one that's older somewhere else. Guinness writes: "The oldest purpose-built cinema in operation was achieved by Plaza 1907, which has been in operation since 22 May 1907."

PLAZA 1907

What: Oldest movie theater in the world

Where: 209 S. Main St., Ottawa, KS 66067

Cost: Entry to the theater's museum is $6 per person. See the website (Plaza1907.com) for movie ticket prices.

Pro Tip: Plan to go early or stay after your film to see the museum behind the big screen.

The theater closed for five years during the Great Depression, but no one ever used the building for anything but showing movies before its reopening in 1934 or after. The current owner, Scott Zaremba, told *Kansas City* magazine that he thinks this theater has survived longer than any other because of the way it was constructed. The walls of the old projection room are steel-lined concrete—most cinema fires started in projection rooms because the film was made of super-flammable nitrate.

Kansas City magazine reports that the first movies shown in the building were *Bad Mother*, *A Trip to the Stars on a Soap Bubble*, and *Two Wives for One Husband*.

The world's oldest movie theater is completely modernized.

In the lobby of the theater is the framed Guinness certificate.

KANSAS AND FRANCE ARE PRETTY MUCH THE SAME

Do utopias ever work out?

Quick, name the silk capital of the United States! That's a tricky question. If you're from the East Coast and especially good with the history of textiles, you probably yelled out "Paterson, New Jersey!" and were right, because for years they did brisk business. These days, no real silk industry exists in the United States, but in the late 1800s, Kansas cranked out a fifth of the country's silk—mostly due to the dreams of one wily Frenchman near Williamsburg, Kansas, in Franklin County. That productivity, along with a first-place ribbon at the Philadelphia Centennial Exposition in 1876, was enough for fabric lovers to bestow on Kansas the nickname "silk-producing capital of America," according to Adrian Zink's *Hidden History of Kansas*.

But who was this Frenchman? He was Ernest Valeton de Boissière (1811–1894). He was not someone interested in going with the flow and actively spoke out against the new emperor, Louis Napoleon. According to an article by R. Alton Lee, Napoleon III told de Boissière it'd be best for the dissident's health if he left the country. Before you knew it, he was setting up Silkville, a utopian society in Kansas. He saw how well mulberry trees grow in these parts

It's unclear if this abandoned building was part of Silkville, but it appears to be the right vintage and is in the right neighborhood.

(silkworms love a good mulberry leaf) and bought up 3,500 acres in 1869. Forty of his compatriots paid $100 each to join him, planted thousands of mulberry trees, imported a bunch of silkworms from Japan, and got to work. By 1872, the workers were turning out 225 yards of silk ribbon every day. As for the utopian part, de Boissière said everyone had to treat each other nicely, which is fine, but in signing on with him, his followers had also agreed to no religion and no marriage. Well, a lot of people like religion and marriage, and the next thing de Boissière knew, the dream was over, and he was back in France. When he was an old man, he returned to Kansas and donated his property to the Independent Order of Odd Fellows so they could make it into an orphanage. Nowadays, the property is a working cattle ranch owned by Bichelmeyer Meats.

Workers made cheese and wine, and the property opened for tours on certain Sundays. But, toward the end of his enterprise, the whole silk industry tanked, which no amount of wine and cheese could make up for, but it helped.

183

MORE DOLLARS THAN YOU CAN SHAKE A RIB AT

Is there room for mine?

During some downtime nine years ago, employees at Guy & Mae's Tavern made a paper airplane out of a dollar bill. Someone threw it, and its nose stuck in the metal of one of the light fixtures over the bar. Since it was a funny fluke, owner Lori Thompson left it where it was. But at some point, a customer noticed it and wanted to see if he could make one stick, too. Before long, more customers thought it'd be fun to decorate the tiny barbecue restaurant with dollars. Now nearly every inch of the place is covered with a bill, most of them marked with names, dates, or messages about anniversaries and birthdays. The tradition is so strong that Thompson, granddaughter of founders Guy and Mae Kesner, keeps markers and tape on the bar. With most of the wall space gone, those eager to leave their mark have started hanging dollars from the acoustic ceiling tiles.

Guy & Mae's is positioned just off of old Highway 50, a scenic, historic route that runs from Ocean City, Maryland, to West Sacramento, California. It's 3,000 miles long and mostly runs through rural areas—*Time Magazine* nicknamed it the "Backbone of America" in a 1997 article. Check out route50.com for more information about the entire route as well as specific spots in Kansas and Missouri that might interest you.

The Kesners opened the bar in 1973 in the building that also houses Williamsburg City Hall.

GUY & MAE'S TAVERN

What: A great place for barbecue, heavily decorated in dollar bills

Where: 119 W. William St., Williamsburg, KS 66095

Cost: The menu is simple and pricing is modest, but be aware that they only accept cash.

Pro Tip: While you're in town, go across the street to the park and visit the statue of town founder William Schofield.

Top: Nearly every inch of the tavern is covered in dollar bills.

Bottom: Looking at it from the outside, you might not even know it's open. It's surprisingly warm and inviting on the inside, though.

GHOSTS LIKE WINE TOO

Is it possible to be too spooked to want a drink?

It's a pity that a place founded on all the best humankind can offer would turn so scary in later years. However, from the legion of poison ivy plants at attention around the abandoned buildings, to the dark, staring windows of an excellent events space and inn, the Belvoir Winery property in Liberty, Missouri, is frightening. Throughout the first half of the twentieth century the building housed orphans, and who can say the words "housed orphans" without a twinge of panic? The Missouri lodge of the Independent Order of Odd Fellows (a benevolent fraternal order) built the complex as a sort of insurance policy for its members, as the Belvoir website explains. Rather than allow an orphaned child, a penniless widow, or an aged parent to wind up homeless, the Odd Fellows knew they could count on their club to care for those they loved. But no place that teemed with unfortunate souls for so many years could just suddenly rest, could it? The complex is definitely haunted, and Belvoir is the first to admit it—the winery hosts a paranormal prom and paranormal investigations of the property, and national television shows have featured its spookiness.

In 2017, operating manager Jesse Leimkuehler told the *Kansas City Star* that staff members hear running, laughing, and objects moving around with no explanation. He said staff and

BELVOIR WINERY

What: Haunted orphanage-turned-winery

Where: 1325 Odd Fellows Rd., Liberty, MO 64068

Cost: Free to stop by, but the wine'll cost you.

Pro Tip: No kidding—really watch out for the poison ivy if you decide to walk around the buildings.

The foreboding entrance alone might give you goosebumps.

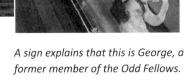

A sign explains that this is George, a former member of the Odd Fellows.

guest reports of adult-sized ghosts disappearing around corners are common as well. Then there's George the Skeleton. A sign over his glass-encased remains explains that he was an Odd Fellow who died in the 1880s and donated his body, such as it was, to science. Then, when the scientists were done with him, they returned him to the lodge, per his request, so he could continue to participate in a ritual illustrating to new members that they are, indeed, merely mortal. All Odd Fellows lodges have skeletons (Belvoir's sign says most are named George), sometimes papier-mache, sometimes bona fide bone.

Belvoir's wine is really good. Try the red called "Boo's," a rich nod to traditional port.

SOURCES

Imagine a World without Squirrels
http://archive.oah.org/special-issues/teaching/2013_12/article.pdf
https://www.washingtonpost.com/local/americas-city-squirrels-have-humans-to-thank-
    for-giving-them-a-home/2014/04/05/e0786c20-ba8e-11e3-9a05-c739f29ccb08_story.
    html
https://archive.org/stream/williamrockhilln00camb/williamrockhilln00camb_djvu.txt
https://shsmo.org/sites/default/files/pdfs/kansas-city/kimball/Haskell-2008-04-10.pdf

Dickey's Jealous Rage Births University Building
https://info.umkc.edu/unews/scofield-hall-is-a-former-mansion/

Cool Rocks, Bro
Interview with University of Missouri-Kansas City historian Chris Wolff and https://info.
    umkc.edu/news/lost-art-of-umkc/
https://kcfountains.wordpress.com/2015/06/28/three-graces-fountain/

A Mural That Must Have a Magnetic Pull
Interview with University of Missouri-Kansas City historian Chris Wolff
https://www.umkc.edu/news/posts/2018/november/history-of-haag-hall-don-quixote-
    mural-luis-quintanilla.html

Heads of State Have It Good in Kansas City
https://history.state.gov/departmenthistory/visits/

Statues without Limitations
https://ny.curbed.com/2017/11/7/16616314/old-penn-station-history-photos-mckim/
https://www.brooklynmuseum.org/exhibitions/sculpture_garden/

Bird Lady of Brookside
https://www.kcur.org/post/heres-whats-bird-lady-statue-kansas-citys-brookside-
    neighborhood#stream/0/
https://www.kcur.org/post/saga-brooksides-bird-lady-continues-ring-cat-
    figurines#stream/0/

Horses Have a Powerful Thirst
Piland, Sherry, and Ellen J. Uguccioni. *Fountains of Kansas City: a History and Love Affair.*
    Kansas City, MO: City of Fountains Foundation, 1985.

The Badass Conley Sisters
https://digitalcommons.law.yale.edu/cgi/viewcontent.cgi?article=1110&context=yjlf
https://umkc.app.box.com/s/k4tek46kysdpft1d698ad8jyyfizgrc5?utm_
    source=KC+History+Tastemakers&utm_campaign=86202a96bc-EMAIL_
    CAMPAIGN_2020_01_02_05_26&utm_medium=email&utm_term=0_da78e63be8-
    86202a96bc-150199825&mc_cid=86202a96bc&mc_eid=203c4d6747
https://scholars.fhsu.edu/cgi/viewcontent.cgi?article=1030&context=theses

Largest Iron for Miles Around
https://www.wycokck.org/WycoKCK/media/Urban-Planning-Land-Use/Documents/
    Historic-Landmarks.pdf
https://sillyamerica.com/blog/large-sculpture-of-an-old-fashioned-iron/

This Ain't Your Kennedy Curse
https://ohiohistorycentral.org/w/Tenskwatawa

Forget Potholes—This Street Will Really Wreck Your Tires
Penner, Marci, and WenDee Rowe. *The Kansas Guidebook 2: for Explorers*. Inman, KS: Kansas Sampler Foundation, 2017.

Swings Just Aren't Enough for Some Kids
"Cannon in Shawnee Park." The Kansas-City Globe, March 9, 1914.
"This Cannon Went to War Again." The Kansas-City Globe, January 31, 1946.

The Pyramids of Pump Station #39
Local Kansas City History Buffs Facebook page: https://www.facebook.com/groups/126159798374

Mystery of the Rosedale Gargoyles
https://www.westwoodks.org/vertical/Sites/%7B15EFBA29-5AD1-451A-8674-DF587143350D%7D/uploads/ROSEDALEARCH.pdf

A Prison Fit for a Princess
https://www.kcur.org/show/central-standard/2014-07-24/what-is-that-kansas-citys-vine-street-castle
https://www.kansascity.com/news/business/development/article236870868.html

Charlie Parker's Challenging Memorialization
https://www.mentalfloss.com/article/500638/grave-sightings-charlie-parker
https://www.birdlives.co.uk/the-end-and-after-1

Going to Kansas City
https://www.kcur.org/arts-life/2016-05-16/news-flash-to-the-world-kansas-city-has-no-12th-street-and-vine-heres-why
https://kcparks.org/places/goin-to-kansas-city-plaza-at-twelfth-street-and-vine/
https://www.thepitchkc.com/take-note/

Walt Disney Didn't Invent Mickey Mouse
https://thankyouwaltdisney.org/history
Ryan, Jeff, and Roger Langridge. *A Mouse Divided: How Ub Iwerks Became Forgotten, and Walt Disney Became Uncle Walt.* New York, NY: Post Hill Press, 2019.

Wealthiest Black Girl in the Nation
Bolden, Tonya. *Searching for Sarah Rector.* New York: Abrams Books for Young Readers, 2014.
https://pendergastkc.org/article/biography/sarah-rector

Arthur Kraft, Forever
https://www.kcur.org/arts-life/2019-07-12/new-fans-try-to-revive-the-legacy-of-a-once-great-mostly-forgotten-kansas-city-artist

No One Wants to Burn Bridges
https://www.kansascity.com/news/your-kcq/article229069344.html

President Truman Was Pretty Hard to Follow
https://www.politico.com/story/2018/11/02/truman-defeats-dewey-1948-950635
https://www.trumanlibrary.gov/education/student-resources/places/the-elms-hotel
https://www.chicagotribune.com/nation-world/chi-chicagodays-deweydefeats-story-story.html

https://time.com/3879744/dewey-defeats-truman-the-story-behind-a-classic-political-photo/

https://www.history.com/news/dewey-defeats-truman-election-headline-gaffe

https://www.kansascity.com/news/local/article19107345.html

No, Not That IHOP

https://www.ihopkc.org/

https://www.womenofgrace.com/blog/?p=51406

https://www.thepitchkc.com/former-ihop-member-explains-why-he-left-the-church/

https://talkingpointsmemo.com/longform/inside-the-international-house-of-prayer--2

http://www.mikebickle.org.edgesuite.net/MikeBickleVOD/2008/20081230A_Forerunner_Ministry-_Preparing_for_the_Day_of_the_Lord_ETP05.pdf

http://www.charismamag.com/spirit/prophecy/38598-mike-bickle-we-believe-part-of-this-bob-jones-prophecy-will-come-to-pass-this-week

Hey, That Buffalo Mantelpiece Belongs to Me!

https://www.mentalfloss.com/article/502461/you-could-once-buy-%E2%80%9Cmemento-kits%E2%80%9D-made-white-house-scraps

Photo permissions: https://www.trumanlibrary.gov/photograph-records/62-652

An English Cow . . . with a Past

https://books.google.com/books?id=k1UaAAAAIAAJ&pg=PA424&lpg=PA424&dq=why+was+the+cow+named+anxiety&source=bl&ots=J9VIKg7Xxp&sig=ACfU3U3NdT8O5W888G8tb9bLWne4UMcdAQ&hl=en&sa=X&ved= 2ahUKEwi7jZKjt_XnAhXMvJ4KHe9RA54Q6AEwD3oECAkQAQ#v= onepage&q=anxiety&f=false

https://www.thecattlesite.com/breeds/beef/14/hereford

https://hereford.org/wp-content/uploads/2017/02/issue-archive/0708_Legends.pdf

https://www.examiner.net/article/20140313/blogs/303139986

Come a Little Bit Closer to KC; It's Better Here

Gilpin, William. Mission of the North American People: Geographical, Social, and Political. New York: Da Capo, 1974. Available online at: https://quod.lib.umich.edu/m/moa/abl0942.0001.001/1?q1=missouri&view=image&size=100

Finally, a Cure for Everything

https://cityofesmo.com/index.php/hall-of-waters/

http://www.exsmo.com/comhistory_overview.html

I Love You Locks

https://www.kansascity.com/news/local/article60265491.html

https://www.kansascity.com/news/local/article131979444.html

https://missourilife.com/old-red-bridge/

https://kcparks.org/places/old-red-bridge-love-locks/

Exchange Students on the Range

https://www.flatlandkc.org/news-issues/preserve-species-eat/

Penguins and Elephants Live in Harmony

https://www.kcur.org/show/central-standard/2014-09-10/the-story-behind-the-giant-fiberglass-penguin-at-kansas-citys-penguin-park

George Park, the Man with Nine Lives

https://kchistory.org/week-kansas-city-history/death-takes-holiday-maybe

http://www.freedomsfrontier.org/pages/parkville-stories

City of Caves
https://www.kansascity.com/news/your-kcq/article222846235.html
https://huntmidwest.com/industrial-space-for-lease/what-is-subtropolis/
Entry in *Missouri Curiosities* about this, page 96.
https://www.kansascity.com/news/business/article174590866.html

Treatment or Torture? Oops!
Interview with Kathy Reno
Mostly from conversations with Kathy Reno. Also from research for this article, though
the article doesn't have much to do with the entry: https://www.kcur.org/arts-
life/2019-05-27/st-josephs-psychiatric-museum-lets-visitors-pretend-to-be-detectives-
like-on-tv

Fertile Land That First Fed the Insane Went on to Grow Superbowl Champs
https://dnr.mo.gov/shpo/nps-nr/08001386.pdf
https://www.missouriwestern.edu/about/wp-content/uploads/sites/12/2017/06/
    FlanaganBook.pdf
http://www.asylumprojects.org/index.php/St._Joseph_State_Hospital

Bonnie and Clyde Detail Gone Awry in Hollywood
https://fox4kc.com/2019/07/19/decades-ago-bonnie-and-clyde-had-one-of-their-most-
    notorious-gunfights-here-in-kc/

A Doll for Every Occasion
https://www.ufdc.org/

Heart of America, Writ Large in Wood
https://www.amusingplanet.com/2016/10/8-living-memorials-shaped-out-of-trees.
    html#:~:text=Heart%2DShaped%20Forest,of%20heart%20failure%20in%201995.
https://www.kansascity.com/news/your-kcq/article236589268.html

Life-Sized Calendar Invented by Ancient Humans
https://www.csmonitor.com/1983/0818/081847.html
See also: https://en.wikipedia.org/wiki/Cahokia_Woodhenge

A Nice Mama Ghost
http://www.wornallmajors.org/explore/wornall-house/
Bruce, Janet. *The John Wornall House 1858: The History and Restoration of Kansas City's
    Historic Wornall House Museum*. Lowell Press: 1983.

A Hill That Isn't a Hill
https://www.indianmoundneighborhood.org/indian-mound/?fbclid=IwAR3vBsANCdiFgfxS
    FX5dni_cgHQM-_ApEEqkiVcKXfnLn8tpF7GuLr556aw
https://www.smithsonianmag.com/history/white-settlers-buried-truth-about-midwests-
    mysterious-mound-cities-180968246/

The True Tale of a Truck-Eating Bridge
https://www.kshb.com/news/region-missouri/jackson-county/trucks-keep-slamming-into-
    a-northeast-kansas-city-bridge
https://www.kctv5.com/news/local_news/low-kcmo-railRd.-bridge-sees-continuous-
    crashes-and-headaches-for/article_24f9f8c4-f476-11e9-bfd9-13661c375ac2.html
https://www.modot.org/sites/default/files/documents/Cost%20Operations%20from%20
    Citizen%27s%20Guide%20to%20Transportation%20Funding%20in%20Missouri-4.pdf

https://www.kcur.org/government/2019-02-20/are-kansas-streets-really-clearer-of-snow-than-missouris-lets-compare-budgets

https://bridgehunter.com/mo/jackson/bh45541/

The Best Ghost You Could Hope to Hang With

Annual Report, Building and Loan Associations by Missouri. Bureau of Building and Loan Supervision (1896-1921).

Dear Abby for the Dead

https://www.oldest.org/sports/mlb-players-ever

https://www.history.com/news/10-things-you-may-not-know-about-satchel-paige

http://mlb.mlb.com/mlb/history/mlb_negro_leagues_profile.jsp?player=paige_satchel

A DIY Flight Simulator!

https://www.rogerdodger.net/builder-academy/

https://atpflightschool.com/become-a-pilot/flight-training/pilot-training-cost.html

https://www.airlinehistory.org/

The Vessel Is Ready; Now We Just Need the Technology

https://www.yesterland.com/moonliners.html

While All the World Is Watching Us, Let's Make Mural History

https://www.kcur.org/post/kansas-city-prepares-solar-eclipse-muralists-make-more-viewing-opportunities

https://www.sprayseemo.com/

This Cow Is All Bull

https://www.kcfountains.com/single-post/2016/09/19/The-Hereford-Bull

https://siris-artinventories.si.edu/ipac20/ipac.jsp?session=159409I8501NC.25930&menu=search&aspect=Keyword&npp=50&ipp=20&spp=20&profile=ariall&ri=&term=hereford+bull&index=.GW&x=15&y=15&aspect=Keyword&term=&index=.AW&term=&index=.TW&term=&index=.SW&term=&index=.FW&term=&index=.OW&term=&index=.NW

The Spot Not Named for Lewis and Clark

https://www.flatlandkc.org/people-places/unknown-monuments-kansas-city/

https://kcparks.org/places/corps-of-discovery/

Jim Pendergast, the Shuffled-Around Brother

https://pendergastkc.org/article/biography/james-francis-pendergast

The Birthplace of Kansas City

http://kchistory.org/faq/are-kansas-city-stockyards-still-open-and-operating

https://livestockexchangebldg.com/available-spaces/

http://livestockexchangebldg.com/history/

https://www.kansascity.com/latest-news/article295396/Last-cattle-auction-at-KC-stockyards.html

https://dnr.mo.gov/shpo/nps-nr/84002571.pdf

A Lot of Trouble for a Low-Visibility Footbridge

https://jessesmall.com/Asset.asp?AssetID=51164&AKey=C782FMSB

Snake Shmake

http://www.theworldslargestsnake.com/

https://fox4kc.com/news/medusa-the-world-record-holding-python-celebrates-15th-birthday-at-kcs-the-edge-of-hell/

https://www.bbc.com/news/world-asia-39427462

https://secure.interactiveticketing.com/1.26/c8816e/#/select

Stay off the Shoulder

https://www.kcur.org/post/one-kansas-city-man-made-it-his-mission-dig-out-forgotten-buried-park#stream/0

http://www.squeezeboxcity.com/lost-in-plain-sight-kansas-citys-west-terrace-park/

The Abduction of Kansas City's Fashion Monarch

https://www.seamwork.com/issues/2015/12/nelly-don-self-made-in-america

https://nellydon.com/blogs/news/the-kidnapping-of-nell-donnelly

https://www.visitkc.com/business-detail/historic-garment-district-museum-kansas-city

Let's Make That Tacky Hill Disappear

Cronkite, Walter. *A Reporter's Life*. New York: Alfred A. Knopf, 1996.

https://www.thepitchkc.com/greetings-from-crown-center-at-40-hallmarks-island-of-misfit-ideas/

https://shsmo.org/sites/default/files/pdfs/kansas-city/kimball/Kipp-04-20-1995.pdf

A Norman Rockwell of Our Own!

https://www.hallmarkartcollection.com/artwork/the-kansas-city-spirit

https://www.hallmarkartcollection.com/creatively-thinking/stories/the-kansas-city-spirit

Sometimes Trees Are Pink

https://www.kcur.org/post/one-kansas-city-artist-open-spaces-means-extra-room-breathe#stream/0

Murder "Mystery" and an Amazing Memorial

https://kchistory.org/week-kansas-city-history/dr-hyde-and-mr-swope

https://www.kcur.org/post/mysterious-death-kansas-citys-thomas-swope#stream/0

https://kchistory.org/week-kansas-city-history/dr-hyde-and-mr-swope

https://kcparks.org/places/swope-park/

Ruins from a Future Civilization

https://www.artskcgo.com/event/architectural-folly-future-place-jill-downen/

https://www.kcur.org/post/kansas-citys-open-spaces-arts-festival-was-last-summer-these-7-pieces-are-still#stream/0

The Park That Just Won't Quit

https://www.onlyinyourstate.com/missouri/kansas-city/kc-aboveground-cave/

https://www.kansascity.com/news/local/article148532679.html

Mausoleums: They're Not Just for The Dead

https://www.waymarking.com/waymarks/WM8T3W_Mount_Moriah_Mausoleum_Kansas_City_Missouri

A Neglected Piece of the White House

https://www.whitehousehistory.org/the-truman-renovation-souvenir-program

Say, Who Invited the Egyptologist?

https://www.metmuseum.org/toah/hd/erev/hd_erev.htm

The Well-Traveled Tree
https://nssdc.gsfc.nasa.gov/planetary/lunar/moon_tree.html

Louisburg: Cider and Apex Predators
http://www.republic-online.com/obituaries/william-billy-dean-pottorff/article_c1f17627-ca5d-5ac3-bdff-d7501399a8e1.html

Missouri's Where It's At
https://www.churchofjesuschrist.org/study/manual/revelations-in-context/far-west-and-adamondiahman?lang=eng&groupid=99274384620923925210-eng

https://www.sos.mo.gov/archives/resources/mormon

All Hail, President Atchison
https://www.senate.gov/artandhistory/history/minute/President_For_A_Day.htm

Kill Creek Isn't That Scary
https://www.kcur.org/talk-show/2019-10-10/kansas-is-haunted-says-this-writer-of-midwestern-gothic-novels

Fictional Tennessee Town with Its Roots in Kansas
https://www.kcur.org/arts-life/2018-12-28/this-lawrence-novelist-just-deepened-the-mysteries-in-the-popular-limetown-podcast

Johnson County's Army Base
https://jocohistory.wordpress.com/2014/02/18/sunflower-army-ammunition-plant-a-city-unto-itself/

https://www.kansascity.com/news/business/article232782032.html

Bricklaying: A Spectator Sport?
https://www.pampamuseum.org/bricklayer-indian-jim.html

https://www.jocogov.org/sites/default/files/documents/CMO/TBT/Jan-Feb%202020%20Best%20Times_Web_Final_0.pdf

Forget Outer Space, He Flew *Here* First
https://www.usatoday.com/story/news/nation-now/2016/12/08/facts-prove-john-glenn-badass/95160148/

https://wingsoverkansas.com/profiles/a1005/

https://www.history.com/this-day-in-history/john-glenn-returns-to-space

https://gardnernews.com/veteran-recalls-heyday-of-olathe-naval-air-station/

https://www.kansascity.com/news/local/community/joco-913/article232824372.html

Think Twice before Showing Off
https://shawneemissionpost.com/2015/08/03/thief-steals-plaque-memorializing-1944-plane-crash-that-merriam-historian-worked-decades-to-have-installed-41423/

https://www.kansascity.com/news/local/community/joco-913/northeast-joco/article4843407.html

Graves to Consider While You Dine
Interview with Craig Crease, Kansas City Area Historic Trails Association

An Invisible Boat Anchored in a Dried-Up Sea
https://www.kshb.com/news/local-news/local-pearl-harbor-survivor-honored-in-mission-kansas

https://shawneemissionpost.com/2013/12/06/for-missions-bob-becker-pearl-harbor-day-is-about-remembering-his-brothers-on-the-uss-arizona-23538/

Kansas's Lone Kentucky Derby Winner

http://www.ha-kc.org/images/associations/90/Historical-Perspective.pdf

http://www.americanclassicpedigrees.com/lawrin.html

Your Local Airplane Salvage Yards

https://www.faa.gov/nextgen/equipadsb/

https://www.ainonline.com/aviation-news/business-aviation/2017-12-26/end-line-bizjets-
beer-cans

https://corporatejetinvestor.com/articles/white-industries-put-up-for-sale-745/

http://www.whiteindustries.com/

https://fox4kc.com/2019/02/27/one-of-the-countrys-largest-aircraft-salvage-yards-calls-
bates-city-home/

I Love This Story So Much, I'll Name a Town after It

https://www.bl.uk/learning/timeline/item126924.html

https://www.onlyinyourstate.com/missouri/kansas-city/near-kc-tiny-towns/

https://en.wikipedia.org/wiki/East_Lynne

Our Radical, Vegetarian Forefathers

https://www.chanute.com/archives/article_fc78ed77-1b13-5c35-abfe-4e757e6ff6aa.html

https://www.kcur.org/post/meet-well-meaning-pioneer-behind-vegetarian-fairy-land-
kansas#stream/0

http://kancoll.org/books/colt/

Oldest Movie Theater in the World

https://plaza1907.com/home-page

https://www.kansascitymag.com/the-oldest-movie-theater-in-the-world-is-in-this-tiny-
kansas-town/

Kansas and France Are Pretty Much the Same

https://bichelmeyermeatskc.com/about/bichelmeyer-land-cattle

https://www.encyclopedia.com/history/dictionaries-thesauruses-pictures-and-press-
releases/silk-culture-and-manufacture

https://www.kshs.org/publicat/history/2000winter_lee.pdf

Zink, Adrian. *Hidden History of Kansas*. Charleston, SC: The History Press, 2017.

More Dollars Than You Can Shake a Rib At

https://unusualplaces.org/u-s-route-50-americas-loneliest-road/

https://www.kansascity.com/living/liv-columns-blogs/chow-town/article16393160.html

https://www.route50.com/kansas.htm

Ghosts Like Wine Too

https://www.kansascity.com/news/local/community/816-north/article179885926.html

http://www.belvoirwinery.com/our-history

https://www.atlasobscura.com/articles/odd-fellows-found-skeletons

INDEX